AMSTERDAM UP CLOSE

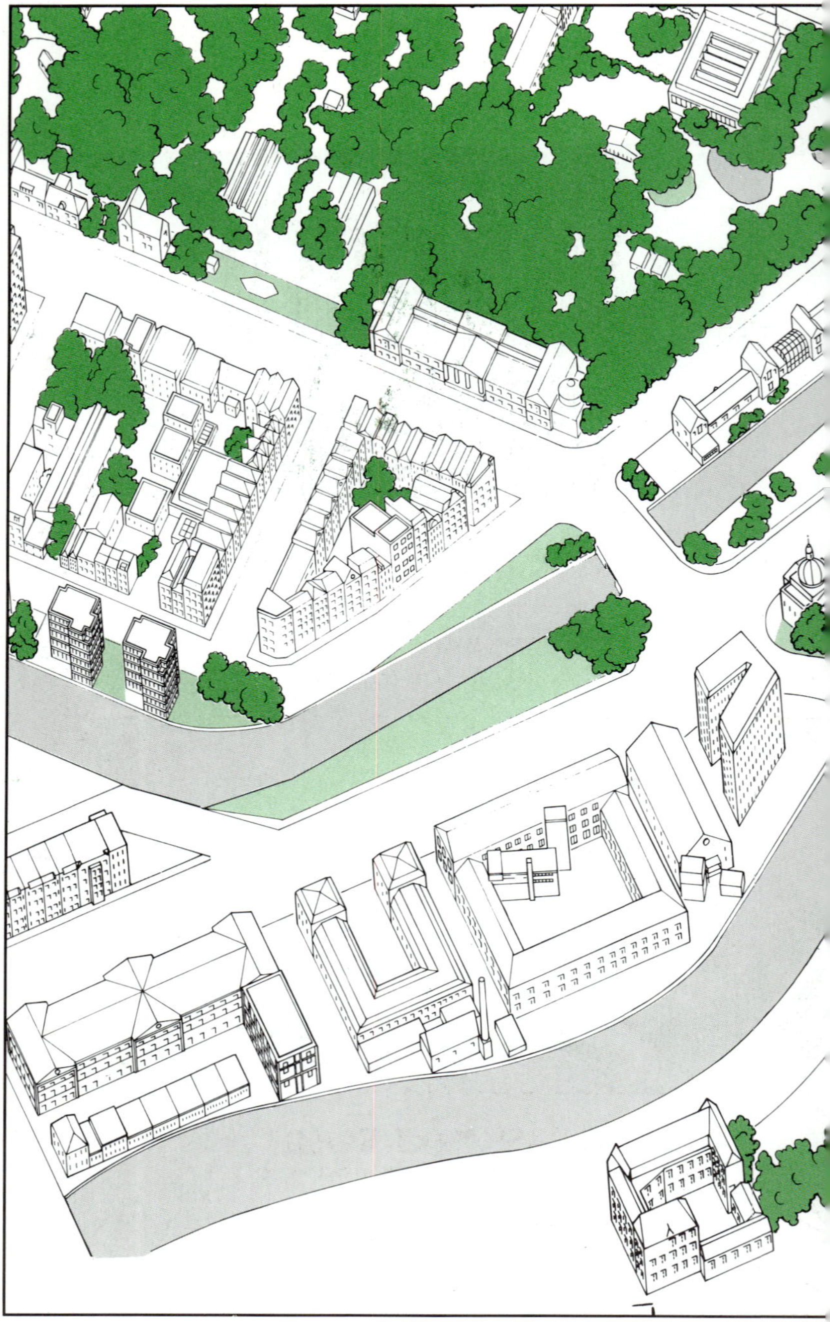

AMSTERDAM UP CLOSE

DISTRICT TO DISTRICT, STREET BY STREET

Written by Fiona Duncan and Leonie Glass
Maps created by Irwin Technical Ltd

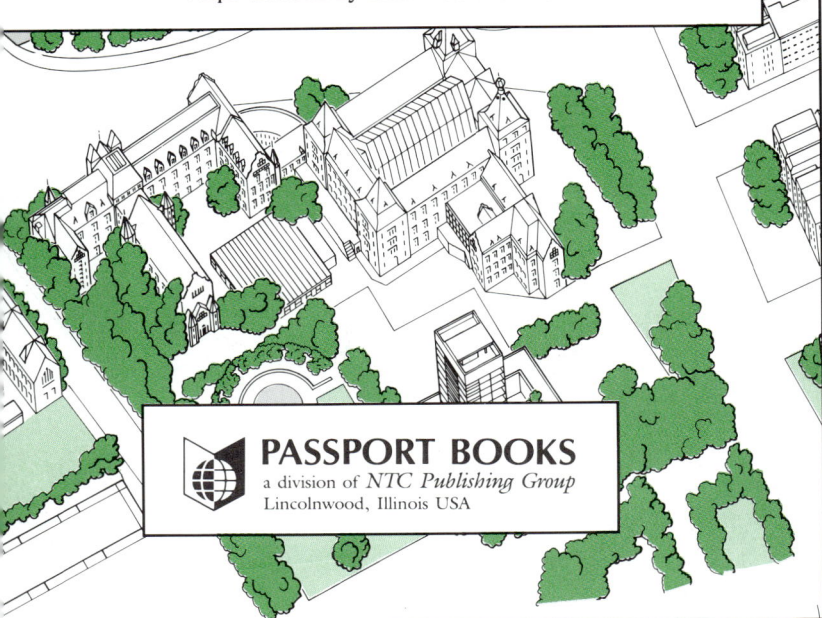

PASSPORT BOOKS
a division of *NTC Publishing Group*
Lincolnwood, Illinois USA

This edition first published in 1993 by Passport Books,
Trade Imprint of NTC Publishing Group, 4255 West Touhy Avenue,
Lincolnwood (Chicago), Illinois 60646-1975 U.S.A.

© Maps Duncan Petersen Publishing Ltd 1993
© Text Fiona Duncan and Leonie Glass 1993

All rights reserved. No part of this publication may be reproduced, stored in a
retrieval system or transmitted in any form, or by any means, electronic,
mechanical, photocopying, recording or otherwise, without prior permission of
NTC Publishing Group.

Conceived, edited and designed by
Duncan Petersen Publishing Ltd,
54, Milson Road,
London W14 0LB

Filmset by SX Composing, Rayleigh, Essex
Printed by Mateu Cromo, Madrid, Spain
Cover photo: Courtesy of the Netherlands Board of Tourism

Every reasonable care has been taken to ensure the information in this guide
is accurate, but the publishers and copyright holders can accept no
responsibility for the consequences of errors in the text or on the maps,
especially those arising from closures, or those topographical changes
occurring after completion of the aerial survey on which the maps are based.

Library of Congress Catalog Card Number: 92-62146

ACKNOWLEDGEMENTS

The authors would like to thank the many people who have helped them with their research, in particular Catherine Palmer, Marianne Wenneker, Els Wamsteeker, Marcel Baltus, Maarten de Sitter, Bart Kraak, and above all Suzanna de Sitter.

Editorial
Editorial director   Andrew Duncan
Assistant editor   Joshua Dubin

Design
Art director   Mel Petersen
Designers   Chris Foley and Beverley Stewart

Aerial survey by KLM Luchtfotografie, Schiphol-Oost, Netherlands
Maps created by Irwin Technical Ltd

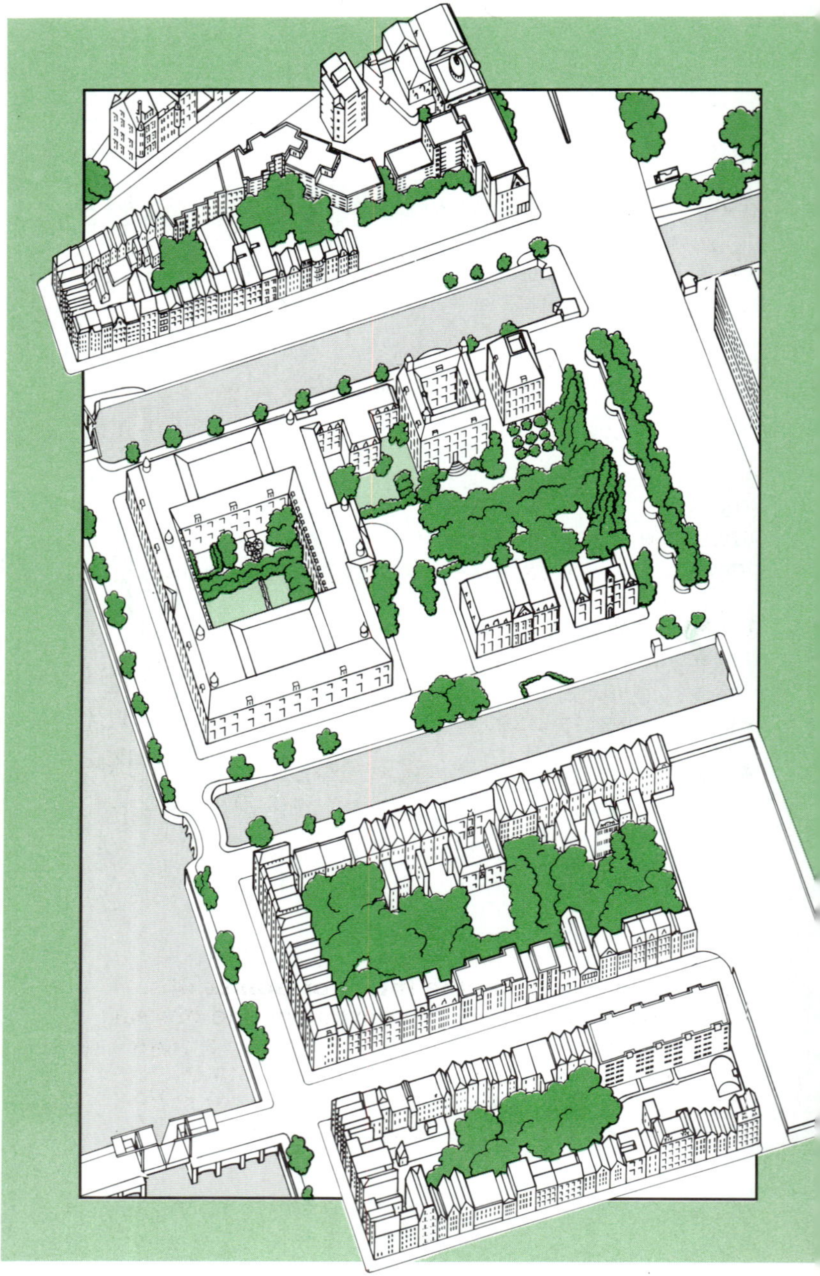

Contents

Acknowledgements	**5**
About this book	**8-11**
Essential information for visitors to Amsterdam	**12-31**
Amsterdam in a nutshell: the sights you should not miss	**14-15**
Master location map	**32-33**
THE ISOMETRIC MAPS	**34-95**
Index of points of interest described in text	**98-117**
Index of people of interest described in text	**118-122**
Index of street names	**123-141**
Amsterdam public transport map	**142-143**

The indexes are essential features of these guides. In particular, the **index of points of interest** provides, under convenient and obvious headings such as shops, museums, cafés, bars and restaurants, a quick-reference listing of essential practical and sightseeing information: instant access to the guide and to the city.

About this book

How the mapping was made

Isometric mapping is produced from aerial photographic surveys. For this book, aerial photography was provided by KLM Luchtfotografie.

Scores of enlargements were made from the negatives, which Irwin Technical, a group of technical illustrators (address on page 5), then used to create the maps. It took well over 1,000 hours to complete the task.

'Isometric' projection means that verticals are the same height, whether in the foreground or the background – at the 'front' (bottom) of the page or at the 'back' (top). Thus the diminishing effect of perspective is avoided and all the buildings, whether near or distant, are shown in similar detail and appear at an appropriate height.

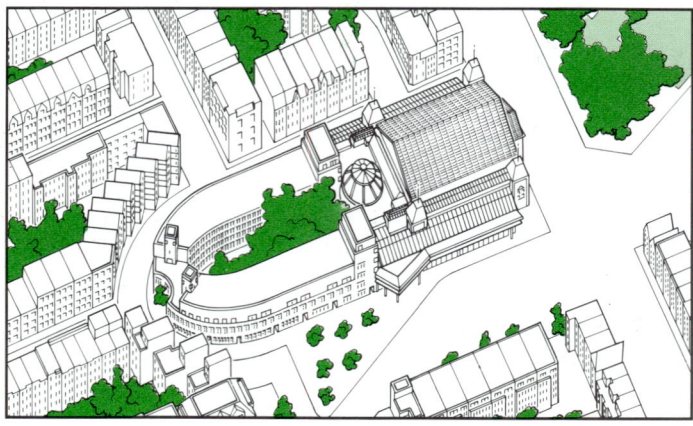

ABOUT THIS BOOK

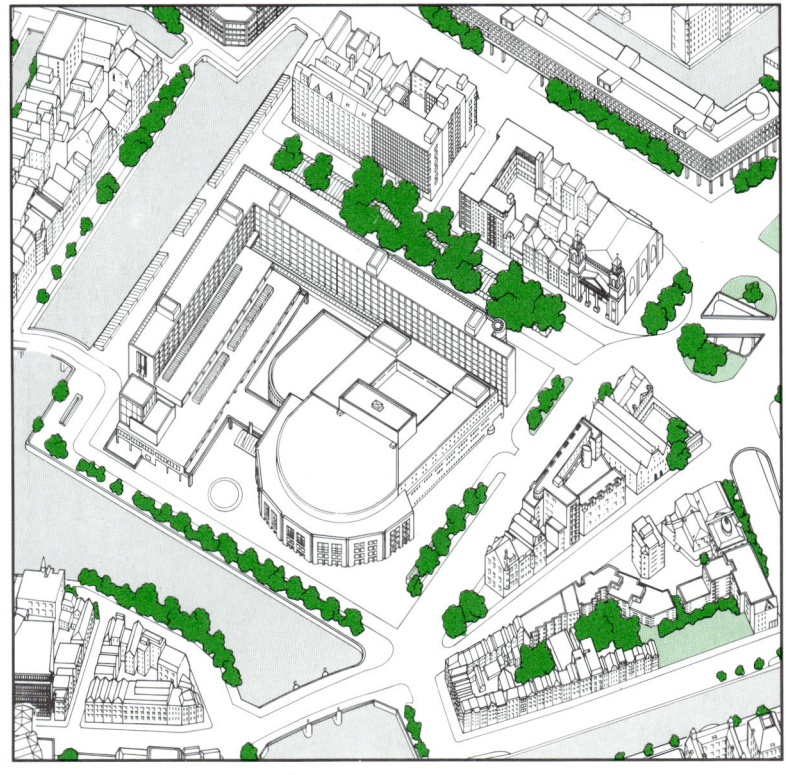

ABOUT THIS BOOK

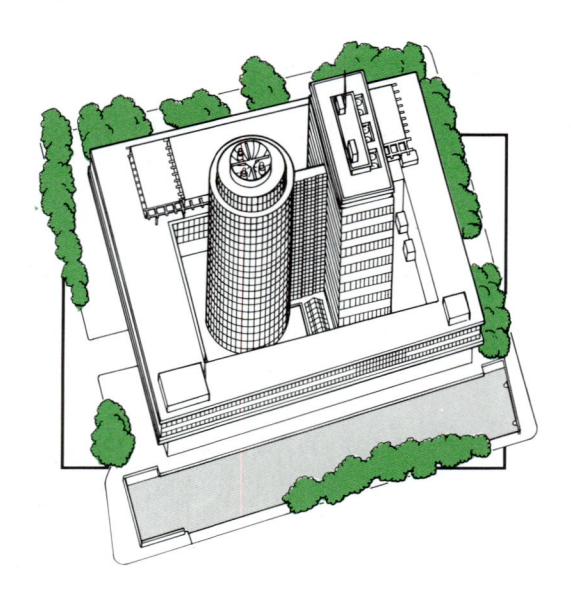

The order of the maps
The map squares are arranged in sequence running from north to south and from west to east. For further details, see the master location map on pages 32-33.

Numerals on maps
Each numeral on a map cross refers to the text printed down the right hand border of the map. The numbers generally read from the top left of each map to the bottom right, in a west-east direction. However, there are deviations from this pattern when several interesting features occur close together, or within one street.

Prices
Restaurants
f means one person can eat for less than 50 guilders (or 'Dutch florins').
ff means one person can eat for less than 100 guilders.

ABOUT THIS BOOK

fff means one person generally pays more than 100 guilders.
   Wine is not included.

Hotels
f means the price per person per night is less than 120 guilders.
ff means the price per person per night is 120-300 guilders.
fff means the price per person per night is more than 300 guilders.

Coverage
No guidebook can cover everything of interest in Amsterdam. This one contains a particularly wide range of information, and the writers have concentrated on aspects of the city brought out by the special nature of the mapping, with emphasis on historical or general information that helps to explain the fabric, evolution and working of the city. They have also tended to draw attention to the outstanding, even the peculiar, sometimes at the expense of the obvious and well-established, in the belief that this best reveals the essential character of a city. There is, in addition, much about eating, drinking, shopping and other practical matters.

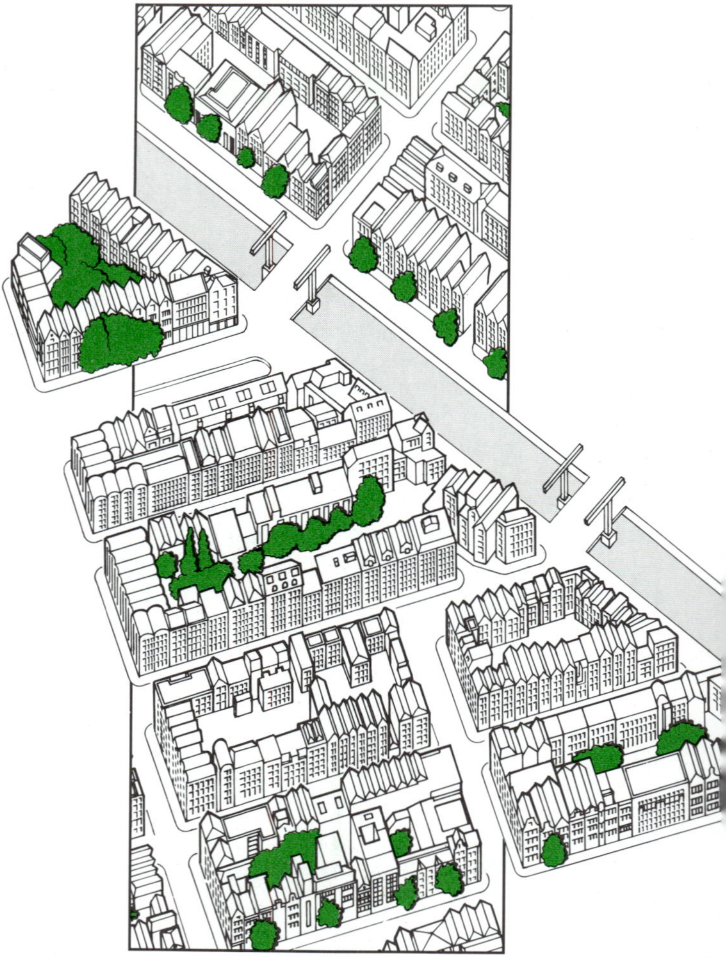

VISITOR INFORMATION

AMSTERDAM IN A NUTSHELL: the sights you should not miss

These two pages give you instant access to the city. Listed are the 'musts' for every visitor to Amsterdam, plus the map pages where you will find the sights marked, together with descriptions linked to the maps by numerals in circles. No such list can pretend to be complete, or to give a fair picture of a city, but if you have limited time, it will help to use this guide to best advantage.

But this book can give you something more than easy access to all the major attractions. The way to get to know a city is, of course, to wander the streets, with no great purpose except to enjoy what comes up. This book is ideal for that, for highlighted on the maps are all the features, well-known and little-known, which make Amsterdam special.

Even if you don't feel like walking, just make your way to one of the map squares, find somewhere comfortable to sit, and 'read' the maps, with their accompanying text: this is as near as you can get to drifting over Amsterdam in a ballon, with your own private guide to describe the points of interest.

Don't miss:

Amstelkring Museum, ⑤, **pages 52-3**, a fascinating glimpse of a 17thC domestic interior, with a Catholic church hidden in the attic. The house incongruously stands in the heart of **De Walletjes**, Amsterdam's seedy but often amusing Red Light District.

Amsterdams Historisch Museum, ④, **pages 60-1**. An excellent place to start your visit, this museum clearly charts the history of Amsterdam, particularly its meteoric rise during the Golden Age of the 17thC.

Anne Frank Huis, ⑥, **pages 48-9**. World famous, yet movingly simple museum dedicated to the memory of the young diarist who hid here with her family for 25 months until discovered by the Nazis and sent to her death.

Begijnhof, ⑤, **pages 60-61**. In the centre of the city, a tranquil and charming courtyard of houses and gardens, first established as a convent in the 14thC. Two churches, one English Reformed and one Catholic, also stand in the square.

Brown cafés are very much part of the Amsterdam scene, and you should experience at least one. Try for example **Hoppe** (⑮, **pages 58-9**), **Het Molenpad** (①, **pages 68-9**), **De Engelbewaarder** (④ **pages 62-3**) or **De Twee Zwaantjes** (①, **pages 48-9**).

Canal boat cruise (for details see the section on 'Essential information'). No trip to Amsterdam is complete without taking one of these.

Grachtengordel. If you have time, the entire C17th canal ring, made up of the Herengracht, Keizersgracht, and Prinsengracht, is worth walking, for there are beautiful buildings and interesting shops and cafés sprinkled all along. However, when time is short, here are suggestions for three parts to explore:

Around Brouwersgracht, ①, **pages 38-9**, at the junction of Prinsengracht, for a feeling of wide open spaces and to see the contrast between a C17th working canal, and a residential one.

Between Radhuisstraat and Leidsegracht, pages 48-49 and 58-59, the little streets which cross from Prinsengracht to Herengracht in this area are full of idiosyncratic shops and good restaurants, and there are plenty of bridges on which to stand and gaze at the lovely canalside houses and mansions.

Along Herengracht from Huidenstraat to Leidsestraat, ⑨, **pages 58-59 and 70-71**. An exceptionally beautiful stretch, whith a string of lovely buildings beginning with the Bijbels Museum. Further on is the much-vaunted Gouden Bocht (①, **page 71**).

Jordaan, **pages 40-1, 46-7**. The humble, industrial district, criss-crossed by little streets and narrow canals, and full of vitality.

Leidseplein, ⑩, **pages 68-9**. Like **Dam Square** (⑧, **pages 50-1**), this is a focal point in the city. This is the entertainment centre, beseiged by cafés, restaurants, bars and nightclubs, theatres and cinemas, and enlivened by street performers at all times of the day and night.

Rembrandthuis, ⑩, **pages 62-3**. The house Rembrandt occupied during his heyday, now filled with his etchings.

Rijksmuseum, ③, **pages 84-5**. The municipal art museum, housing a magnificent collection of Dutch 17thC art, including many Rembrandts and several Vermeers.

Rijsttafel. Indonesian food is a speciality in Amsterdam, and the highlight of the menu is the feast of many dishes called *rijsttafel*. Try Cilubang (**page 59**), Kantjil en de Tijger (**page 61**), Sama Sebo (⑦, **pages 84-5**) or Speciaal (③, **pages 40-1**).

Stedelijk Museum, ①, **pages 94-5**. The liveliest of Amsterdam's three great art museums, the Stedelijk is devoted to modern art.

Van Gogh Museum, ⑧, **pages 82-3**. A permanent home for hundreds of paintings, drawings and letters of Van Gogh, as well and for work by contemporary artists.

VISITOR INFORMATION

Transport

From the airport to the city
It is only an 18-minute train journey from the Schiphol international airport to Amsterdam's Centraal Station or seven minutes to Zuid WTC station and ten minutes to RAI station. This is a frequent and efficient service, with four trains running each hour and, at night, one per hour to Centraal Station only. The KLM Hotel Bus Service takes approximately 30 minutes and operates from the airport to either Centraal Station or Dam Square, stopping off at major hotels on the way. This may prove a viable alternative if you arrive during rush hour when the trains can be congested. In spite of its name, any airline passenger may use this service. Taxis provide an alternative and are readily available, but inevitably more expensive - approximately 50f.

Officially, you are requested to register with the police if you intend to stay more than eight days. If you are staying in a hotel this will be done for you automatically.

Arriving by ferry
It takes about one and a half hours to transfer from the ferry terminal at the Hook of Holland to Amsterdam by either road or rail.

VISITOR INFORMATION

Geography
Your understanding of the geography of Amsterdam will be made easier if you know something of how it evolved. The city's origins were inauspicious, to say the least: a 13thC settlement of fishermen on the marshy and flood-prone banks of the River Amstel. Existence was only made possible by the construction of dykes, and so began the brilliant series of manoeuvres employed through the centuries to tame and utilize the encroaching sea. The dam which was soon built across the Amstel gave the growing town its name.

The 17thC was Amsterdam's Golden Age. Now the city fanned out from Dam, Oude Zijde (Old Side) and Nieuwe Zijde (New Side) with the construction of the great Grachtengordel (Canal Ring), made up of the Herengracht (Gentlemen's Canal), Keizersgracht (Emperors' Canal) and Prinsengracht (Princes' Canal). True to The Netherlands' special status as an 'elected monarchy', the city's burgers, led by the Burgomaster, considered gentlemen to be more important than mere kings and princes, and so the Herengracht was the most prestigious of the three canals. Today these three beautiful waterways still dominate the layout of the city and are the reason for its special appeal. In the 19thC, further expansion pushed the city across the outer canal, the Singelgracht. Nevertheless, Amsterdam remains small-scale: charming, creative and youthful.

Travelling in Amsterdam
The GVB (transport authority) controls an integrated and highly efficient transport system which runs throughout Amsterdam. It operates an uncomplicated tram, bus and metro service. However it is unlikely that you will need the metro as it serves the suburbs only. Taking the tram, cycling and using the canals are all experiences not to be missed on a visit to the city.

Trams and buses
A large proportion of the bus and tram routes begin at Centraal Station but if you wish to start your

17

VISITOR INFORMATION

journey along the route the yellow signs at tram and bus stops are easily seen and clear maps indicating the rest of the route are displayed at the stops or on board the bus or tram. Trams are a fast and efficient method of transport - usually at the expense of other traffic on the road which has to move smartly out of the way. To get on or off a tram, press the yellow button by the door of the tram (inside and outside). If you have no ticket, you must purchase one from the driver. Your ticket has to be stamped by the machine which is usually at the back of the tram. The city buses, which are usually maroon, have one door, located near the driver, who will check your ticket.

The main GVB office is opposite Central Station (tel. 6272727), with smaller offices at 15 Leidseplein and at Amstel station. Public transport maps and advice on buying tickets are available from these offices.

Trams and buses run regularly until midnight from 6 am, Mon-Fri, from 6.30 am on Sat, and from 7 am on Sun. After midnight the night buses take over, giving a less frequent service.

Metro
The two metro lines both terminate at Centraal Station and trains run at approximately the same times as those given for trams and buses.

Tickets
Because of the integrated public transport system tickets can be used on buses, trams and the metro throughout the Netherlands. There are several alternatives when buying tickets.

The cheapest way to travel is to buy a strippenkaart (multi-strip ticket) in strips of two, three, six or 10; it is cheapest to buy strips of 15 or even 45. You can buy them from post offices, stations, **VVV** offices or shops which display the strippenkaart symbol. Strips of six or ten can be bought from the bus or tram driver. There is a flat rate of one ticket per journey plus one ticket per zone travelled, and the strip can be used by more than one person provided it is stamped accordingly. The ticket must be stamped by

VISITOR INFORMATION

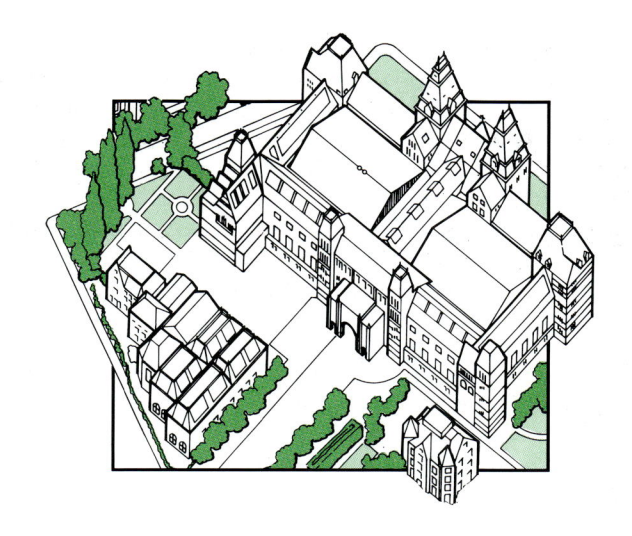

the driver if on a bus or by the machine if on a tram. It will be printed with a time. This entitles the holder to up to one hour's travel, irrespective of any changes or stops needed to complete the journey within the same zone. To go beyond the Centrum zone - which contains most of the places you are likely to visit - you must stamp one extra strip per extra zone. There are frequent ticket inspections, especially on the trams where the onus is on you to stamp your ticket, with on-the-spot fines for those who have failed to do so.

An alternative is a dagkaart which gives unlimited travel for a specified number of days, or an eenrittenkaart which must be bought from the driver for each individual journey. Season tickets are also available from the GVB offices.

Taxis

Taxis can be hailed in the street unless they are within walking distance of one of the ranks located in major squares and by stations and hotel areas. Alternatively telephone 6777777 to order one - it will arrive within minutes. The metered charge will include service, but a tip is always welcome.

VISITOR INFORMATION

By car

Driving a car in Amsterdam, whether your own or rented, is extremely hazardous. Negotiating the narrow, often cobbled, streets seething with pedestrians and cyclists, dodging the trams and avoiding driving into the canals (not an uncommon event in Amsterdam) is not to be recommended. Parking places are also difficult to find, but if you do have a car it is best to park it outside the centre at RAI, Europaboulevard or centrally in a multi-storey car park with security guards, such as Bijenkorf, Beursplein or Europaparking, 250 Marnixstraat; or Muziektheater, Waterlooplein.

In The Netherlands, traffic follows the right-hand side of the road. The speed limit is 50 kph (31 mph) in residential areas but is often further restricted to a crawl. Trams have priority, as do cyclists on the inside lane, and you must give way to traffic coming from the right unless otherwise indicated.

A recent referendum suggested that the citizens of Amsterdam wanted the centre of their city declared a car-free zone. However, so few people voted that no plans to act on the referendum have yet been made.

By bicycle

One of the most enjoyable ways of seeing Amsterdam is to join the throng and travel by bike. Cycling is an art form in itself in Holland, and the Dutch are adept at coolly avoiding the onslaught of trams, buses, cars and pedestrians whilst hardly looking up to see where they are going. Everyone rides a bike in Amsterdam, with their shopping, dogs, babies, girlfriends, perched behind or in front. Not surprisingly there are clearly marked bicycle lanes everywhere and the driving and pedestrian public are reasonably alert to bicycles. Trams, however, will not stop unless absolutely necessary. There are several bicycle hire companies offering reasonable rates including Damstraat Rent-a-bike (11 Pieter Jacobszdwarstraat; tel. 6255029; and 247 Damrak; tel. 6223207) and Macbike (116 Nieuwe Uilenburgerstraat; tel. 6200985); also Take-a-Bike (12 Stationsplein; tel. 6248391).

VISITOR INFORMATION

By canal
No trip to Amsterdam would be complete without seeing the city from the water. The **VVV** have information on canal cruises (see **Sightseeing Tours**, below) but the canals also offer an alternative route for getting around.

The Canal bus, operating 10 am-6 pm at 45-minute intervals, runs between the Rijksmuseum and Centraal Station and stops at Westerkerk/Anne Frank's House, Leidsestraat/Keizersgracht and Leidseplein.

Metered water taxis, providing room for up to seven people, operate as any normal taxi would. They must be ordered by telephone (tel. 6222181) and will collect and drop you at the place of your choice.

During the summer months (Apr-Sep) it is also possible, and great fun, to rent water bicycles for two or four people at a time and explore the canals on your own. Remember to keep to the right hand side. Canal Bike (tel. 6265574) and Röell Canal Boats (tel. 6929124) have several moorings on the main canals and the Amstel.

Railways
If you plan to travel by rail within the Netherlands it may be worth getting a **Holland Rail Pass**, giving foreign visitors unlimited first class travel for three days within a 15-day period. This is available from the GVB or from The Netherlands Board of Tourism in your country of origin. Alternatively, Netherlands Railways offer several day-trip tickets (*dagtochten*) which include train, boat or bus fares and admission fees. These trips operate mostly May-Sep. Another option, if you are travelling extensively within the Netherlands, is to purchase a **Holland Leisure Card** either at the **VVV** or from the Dutch tourist authority in your country of origin. This gives discount on travel, on museum entrances and on some accomodation but you should look into it carefully before purchasing it as it may not prove a wothwhile investment.

VISITOR INFORMATION

Useful data

Tourist information
The main tourist information offices, known as the **VVV**, are located at:
- 10 Stationsplein (tel. 6266444);
- 106 Leidsestraat.

The Stationsplein office is open Easter-Jun and Sep, Mon-Sat 9 am-11 pm, Sun 9 am-9 pm; Jul-Aug, daily 9 am-11 pm; Oct-Easter, 9 am-5 pm. The Leidsestraat office is open Mon-Sun 12.30 pm-5.30 pm. All correspondence for advance information should be addressed to Postbus 3901, 1001 AS Amsterdam, Netherlands; fax (20) 6252869.

These offices are highly efficient and extremely helpful. Apart from issuing maps and information on both general and more specialized topics in several languages, they will also make reservations for hotel rooms, theatres and excursions, and will change money (although the banks offer the most competitive rate). Alternatively, information on theatre, music and other cultural events is available from AUB Ticketshop (Amsterdam's Uit Buro), 26 Leidseplein (tel. 6211211) and they can make credit card bookings for seats.

Disabled visitors
Amsterdam, with its narrow, cobbled streets, is not an easy city for the disabled, but the public transport system and most museums are reasonably accessible. The **VVV** and the Netherlands Board of Tourism in your country of origin list hotels, restaurants and other tourist attractions with facilities for the disabled.

Children
Pushing small children in push-chairs is sometimes difficult but for older children the excitement of everyday life in the city makes it a great experience. The **VVV** will give specific advice on children's activities. Children under four travel free and there

VISITOR INFORMATION

are reduced fares for older children on the public transport system.

Publications

What's On In Amsterdam, an inexpensive fortnightly publication by the **VVV**, is readily available and lists a selection of events, as does *Amsterdam This Week*. For a more comprehensive coverage of less mainstream cultural events visit or ring any Uit Buro (see above) or buy *Uitkrant* which is in Dutch but is relatively easy to follow. The many excellent bookshops in Amsterdam stock an interesting range of books in several languages. A guide to book shopping, entitled *Amsterdam, Book Lover's City*, lists the major bookshops.

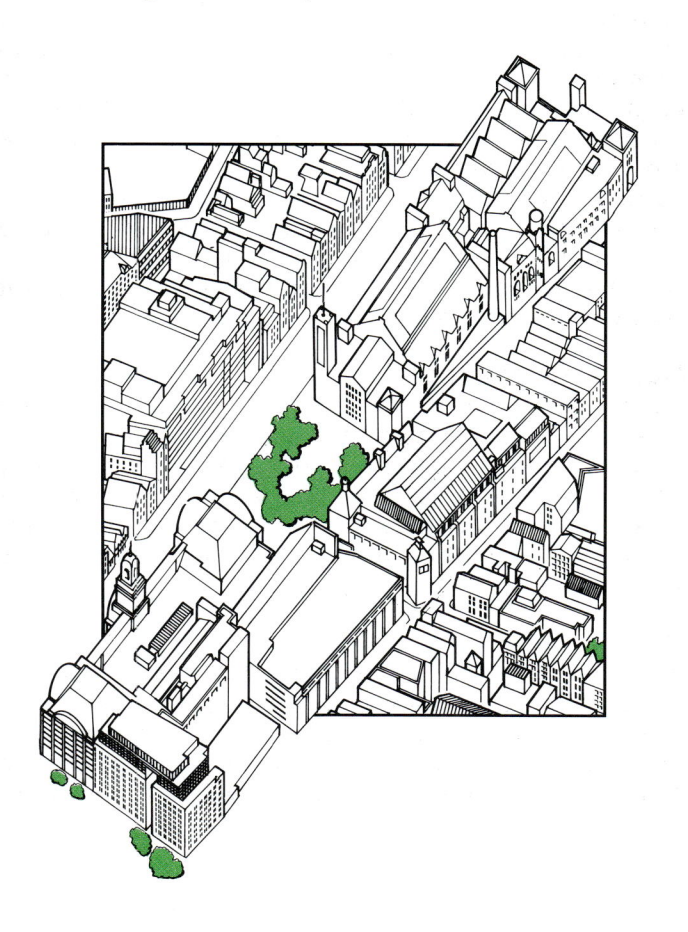

VISITOR INFORMATION

Sightseeing tours

One way to get your bearings when you first arrive in Amsterdam is to take a one-hour guided boat trip run by one of the many tour operators. Tours are plentiful in the summer months and many depart from near Centraal Station and from jetties along the major canals. Some cruises offer a more specialist tour, stopping at selected places or even including dinner. These are listed in the **VVV** publication *Cruises in Amsterdam*. The Touristtram which departs from Centraal Station offers a land-based alternative.

For a more individual tour it is both interesting and enjoyable to take advantage of Amsterdam's compact size and explore by bicycle or on foot. Some bicycle hire companies such as Yellow Bike (66 Nieuwezijds Voorburgwal; tel. 6206940) take guided tours of cyclists. The bicycle hire charge is included in the cost of the tour.

The VVV produces an excellent brochure outlining eight walks covering different aspects of the city and they can recommend several trained guides who will take small groups on walking tours.

If you want to check the accuracy of this guide's mapping, KLM offer a guided tour by helicopter for groups of 10 or 25 (KLM Era Helicopter, PO Box 7700, 1117 ZL Shiphol East; tel. 6492041). It is not cheap.

Museums and other places of interest

Three of the big museums, the Rijksmuseum, the Van Gogh Museum and the Nederlands Scheepvaart Museum are state-run and are open Tue-Sat, 10 am-5 pm, Sun and holidays 1 pm-5 pm, closed Mon. The Stedelijk Museum, the Fodor, the Amsterdams Historisch Museum and the Willet-Holthuysen Museum are municipal museums, open daily 11 am-5 pm, closed 1 Jan. There is an inexpensive entrance charge for all these. The rest are privately owned which means that entrance fees and opening hours are peculiar to each. Many close on Sunday mornings and all of Monday. Churches also have irregular opening hours, depending on when services

VISITOR INFORMATION

are held.

If you plan to visit several museums it is worth buying a Museumjaarkaart which gives free entrance to most museums and reduced entrance to some. This ticket is valid for one year and is available from the VVV who will issue them on the spot - a passport-sized photograph is required.

A happy way of exploring the museums is to use the Museum Boot (Museum Boat), which follows a route between Centraal Station and the Maritime Museum, stopping at Anne Frank's House, Leidseplein, the Rijksmuseum, Herengracht /Leidsestraat and Muziek Theater. The day ticket, available from the **VVV**, or on board the boat, also gives half-price admission to museums along the way.

Here are the opening times of some other interesting museums:

- **Amstelkring Museum**: Mon-Sat 10 am-5 pm, Sun and public holidays 1 pm-5 pm;
- **Beurs van Berlage**: Mon-Sun, 11 am-5 pm;
- **Anne Frank Huis**: Mon-Sat, 9 am-5 pm, Sun and holidays 10 am-5 pm;
- **Joods Historisch Museum**: daily 11 am-5 pm, closed 7 Oct;

VISITOR INFORMATION

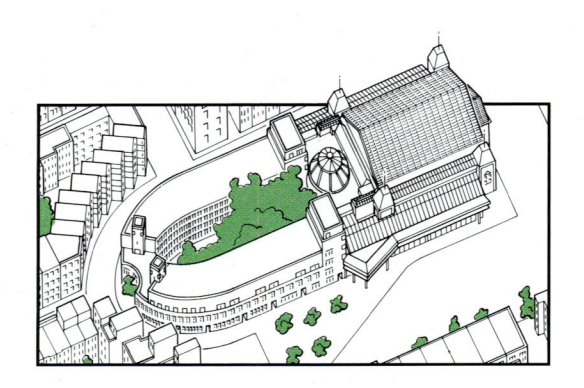

- **Rembrandthuis**: Mon-Sat, 10 am-5 pm, Sun and holidays 1 pm-5 pm;
- **Tropenmuseum**: Mon-Fri, 10 am-5 pm, Sat, Sun and holidays 12 pm-5 pm, closed 30 April, 5 May;
- **Van Loon Museum**: Mon, 10 am-5 pm, Sun 1 pm-5pm.

Shopping, banking and business hours

The large shops tend to keep to regulated opening hours: Mon, 1 pm-6 pm; Tue-Fri, 9 am-6 pm (on Thursday shops stay open until 9 pm); Sat, 9 am-5 pm; closed Sun except for four Sundays a year. Small shops may vary slightly. The markets, too, operate regular hours and the two major ones are open as follows: Albert Cuyp Market, Mon-Sat, 9 am-4.30 pm, and the Bloemenmarkt, Mon-Sat, 9 am-6 pm.

Most banks open Mon-Fri, 9 am-4 pm, with major branches staying open until 7 pm on Thursdays and some open on Saturday mornings as well. The GWK, a national financial body operating at most border posts and stations, operates 24 hours a day at Centraal Station and at Schiphol. Other major branches have longer opening hours than banks. There are many bureaux de change in major tourist

VISITOR INFORMATION

areas and money can also be changed at post offices and at some VVV offices. Exchange rates vary from place to place with banks offering the best rates.

Business hours tend to be approximately 8.30-9 am to 5-5.30 pm, so public transport can be congested at these times.

Public holidays

There are public holidays at Easter, Whitsun and Christmas (see below) and 1 January. The Queen's Birthday (30 April) is the day when Amsterdam lets its hair down. Stalls spring up all over town, selling everything from food to furniture, children play their musical instruments on street corners, and impromptu parties erupt on the streets, especially in the Jordaan. Many shops close again on Remembrance Day (4 May) and Liberation Day (5 May). Throughout June, Amsterdam, along with The Hague, Rotterdam and Utrecht, plays host to the Holland Festival of Music, Opera, Theatre and Dance. On the first Saturday in September there is a spectacular flower procession from Aalsmeer to Amsterdam. On the second Saturday in November St Nicholas, the patron saint of Amsterdam, arrives by steamboat at Centraal Station and parades through the city distributing sweets. On 5 December, when children give and receive small presents, there are great celebrations in preparation for the following day which is St Nicholas's Day (6 December).

Currency

The unit of currency is the guilder (abbreviated in this book to f but also abbreviated to fl, Hfl, Dfl and known internationally as the NLG), and is divided into 100 cents. Coins are in the following denominations: 5 cents (*stuiver*), 10 cents (*dubbeltje*), 25 cents (*kwartje*), 100 cents (*guilder*), f2.5 (*rijksdaalder*) and f5 (five guilders). There are different coloured banknotes, each with embossed markings for the blind, in the following denomininations: 5, 10, 25, 50, 100, 250, 1,000 guilders. Because the 5c piece is the smallest coin prices are often rounded off to the nearest 5c.

VISITOR INFORMATION

Restaurants

Restaurants serving the food of all nationalities abound, including those of former colonies such as Indonesia and Surinam. Don't miss a meal in one of these, and treat yourself to the *rijsttafel*: a traditional feast comprising different dishes served at once. You should also try a traditional Dutch meal at one of the several charmingly old-fashioned Dutch establishments.

The food in newer restaurants is predominantly French. The three-course tourist menu offers sound value in restaurants displaying the knife and fork logo. The Dutch tend to eat a light lunch and many restaurants do not open for lunch. Brown cafés, too, often serve minimal food at lunch, so you may be limited to a broodje (filled roll) from one of the little shops which sell them, and a bag of chips with mayonnaise from a street stall.

Dinner is eaten relatively early, so restaurants are often open by 7 pm, and some have last orders as early as 10 pm. Some restuarants, particularly in the remote areas, are closed on Sundays, and some close on Mondays.

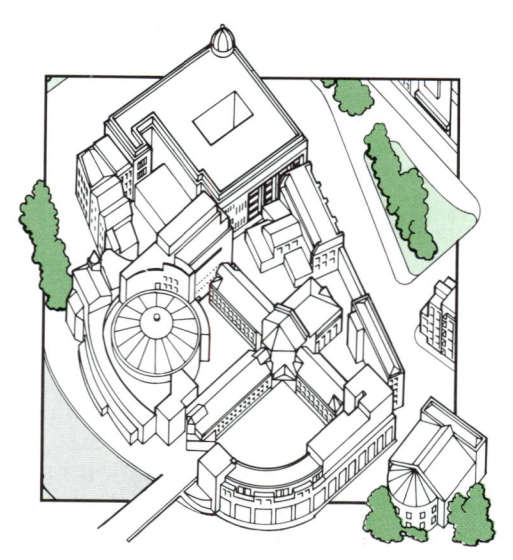

VISITOR INFORMATION

Cafés and bars
Part of the charm of Amsterdam is its traditional brown cafés, so called because of their dark brown walls and simple wooden furnishings. Here you can linger over a book or newspaper (many provide well-lit reading tables), drink a beer or coffee, or eat a light snack. Some date back to the 17thC.

Modern cafés, some of which serve full meals, are known as white or designer cafés. Each year brings a new, fashionable crop.

Also traditional are Amsterdam's proeflokalen or tasting houses. Originally they were attached to jenever (Dutch gin) distilleries, and in them you can still taste the many different types of jenever before, if you wish, purchasing a bottle. There are also a few beer bars, stocking a huge selection of beers.

Post
Post offices marked PTT are normally open Mon-Fri, 8.30 am-5 pm. Also, some are open Sat, 9 am-12 pm. The main post office at 250-256 Singel (tel. 5563311) is open until 8.30 pm on Thur and on Sat, 9 am to noon. Post-boxes are red and marked PTT. Place letters for destinations outside Amsterdam in the slot marked *overige*. Stamps can be bought from post offices and stamp machines (throughout the city), also from shops and news-stands selling postcards.

Telephoning
Green public telephone booths are scattered throughout the city on the streets and in museums and cafés. Alternatively go to Tele Talk Centre (101 Leidsestraat, open 10 am to midnight) or Telehouse (48-50 Raadhuisstraat, open 24 hours) which have facilities for national and international calls, faxes and telegrams. Public telephones take either telephone cards (available from post offices or telephone centres) or 25c coins which is the minimum charge for local calls. Main telephones also take f1 and f2.50 coins, which are needed for international calls. Instructions in several languages

VISITOR INFORMATION

are displayed in the booths but it is important to remember to put some coins in before dialling; more may be inserted during your call. `Partially used' coins will not be returned, so have some small denomination coins ready to feed in towards the end of your conversation. No code is necessary for numbers within Amsterdam. Calls made from hotels can be very expensive.

Time zones
Like most western European countries, The Netherlands is two hours ahead of GMT (Greenwich Mean Time) in the spring and one hour ahead of GMT in the summer.

Foreign embassies
Embassies and consulates are listed in the telephone directory under *Ambassade* and *Consulaat*. Here is a selection:
- **Australia** 23 Koninginnegracht, The Hague; tel. (070) 3630983.
- **Canada** 7 Sophialaan, The Hague; tel. (070) 3614111.
- **France** 2 Vijzelgracht; tel. 6248346.
- **Germany** 172 De Lairessestraat; tel. 6736245.
- **Great Britain** 44 Koningslaan; tel. 6764343.
- **Ireland** 9 Dr Kuyperstraat, The Hague; tel. (070) 3630993.
- **Israel** 47 Buitenhof, The Hague; tel. (070) 3647850.
- **Italy** 609 Herengracht; tel. 6240043.
- **Japan** 50 Vijzelgracht; tel. 6243581.
- **New Zealand** 25 Mauritskade, The Hague; tel. (070) 469324.
- **Spain** 34 Frederiksplein; tel. 6203811.
- **USA** 19 Museumplein; tel. 6645661.

Emergencies
For the fire brigade, police or an ambulance dial the National Emergency Alarm Number, 0611.

VISITOR INFORMATION

Medical emergencies
In case of accident, the following hospitals have casualty departments:
- Academisch Medisch Centrum, 9 Meibertdreef; tel. 5669111.
- Boven't IJ Ziekenhuis, 1 Statenjachstraat; tel. 6346346.
- VU Ziekenhuis, 1117 de Boelelaan; tel. 5489111.
- Lucas Ziekenhuis, 164 Jan Tooropstraat; tel. 5108911.
- Onze Lieve Vrouwe Gasthuis, 197 1e Oosterparkstraat, tel. 5999111.
- Slotervaartziekenhuis, 6 Louwesweg; tel. 5129333.

If you require a doctor or dentist, the Central Medical Service (tel. 6642111) operates 24 hours a day and will refer you to the doctor or dentist on duty.

Late-night pharmacists
The Central Medical Service (tel. 6642111) will also advise on pharmacists open outside shop hours. For prescription drugs you must go to an *apotheek*, and for non-prescription drugs a *drogisterij*.

Main police station
Police: tel. 6222222.
Amsterdam's main police station is at 117 Elandsgracht; tel. 5599111.

Lost property For items lost in the streets try the police lost property office at 11 Waterlooplein (tel. 5598005). For items lost on the tram, bus or metro, go to the GVB office at 108 Prins Hendrikkade (tel. 5514911); for items lost on a train, try Centraal Station (tel. 5578544).

The Amsterdam Tourist Assistance Service (118 Nieuwezijds Voorburgwal; tel. 6239314) offers advice and support on tourist-related emergencies, such as a lost or stolen passport.

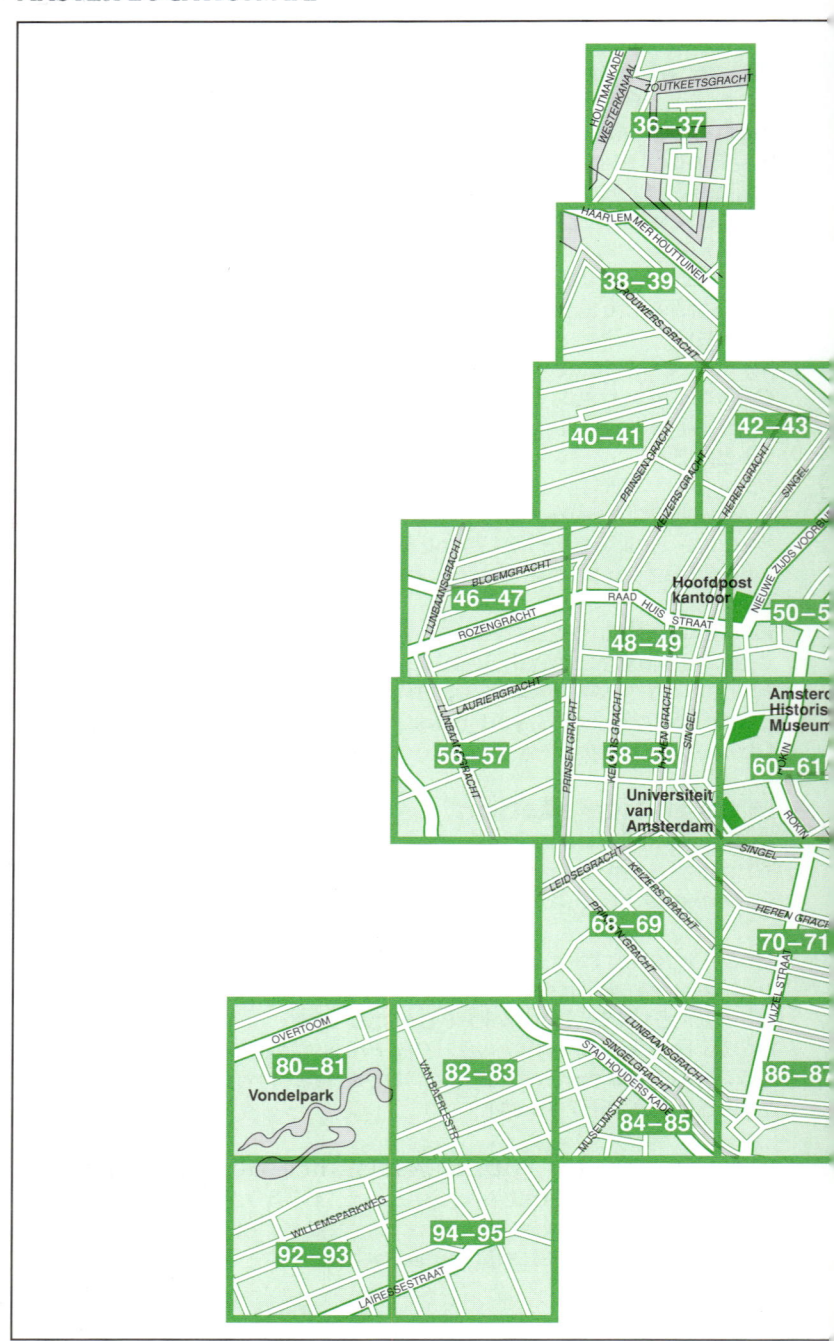

MASTER LOCATION MAP

32

MASTER LOCATION MAP

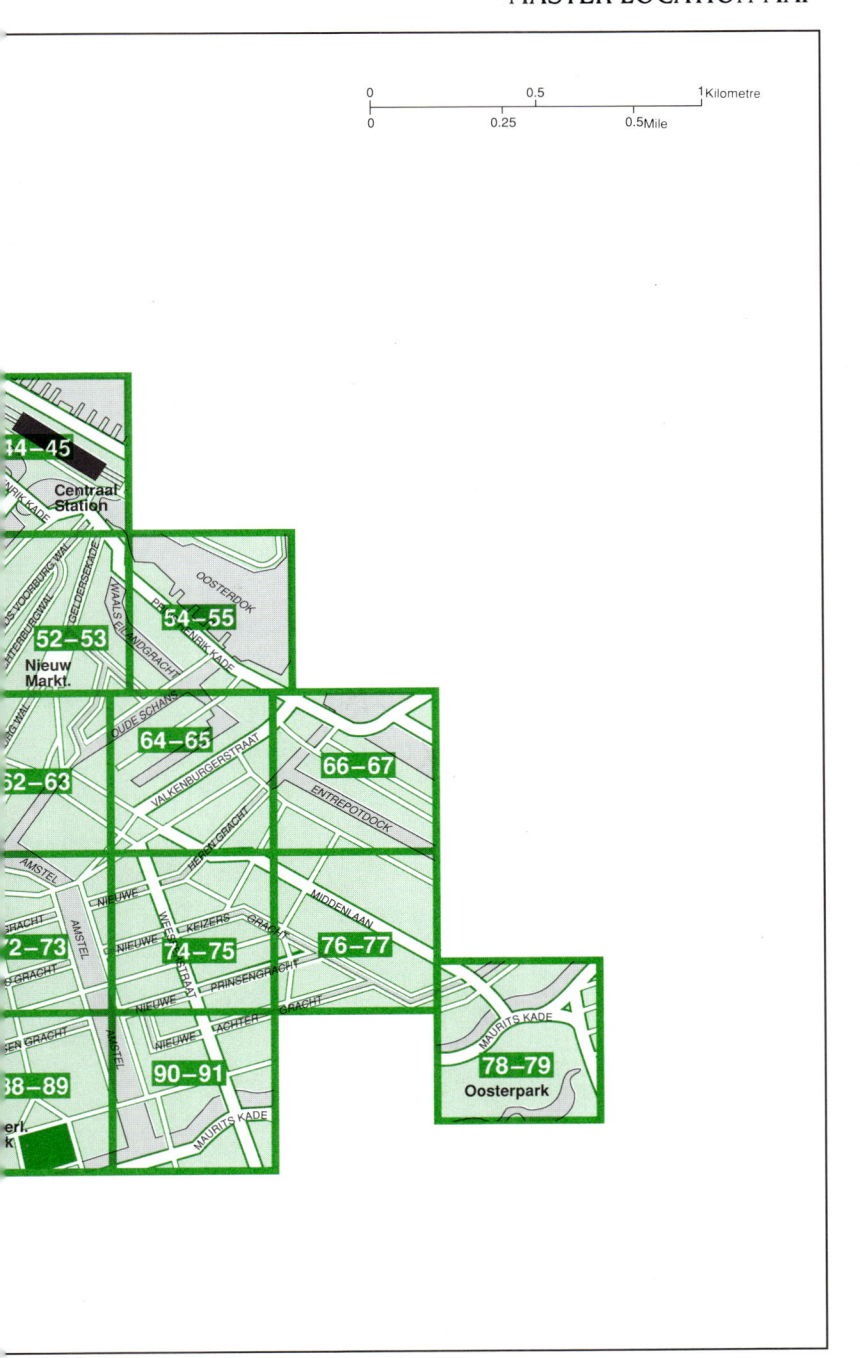

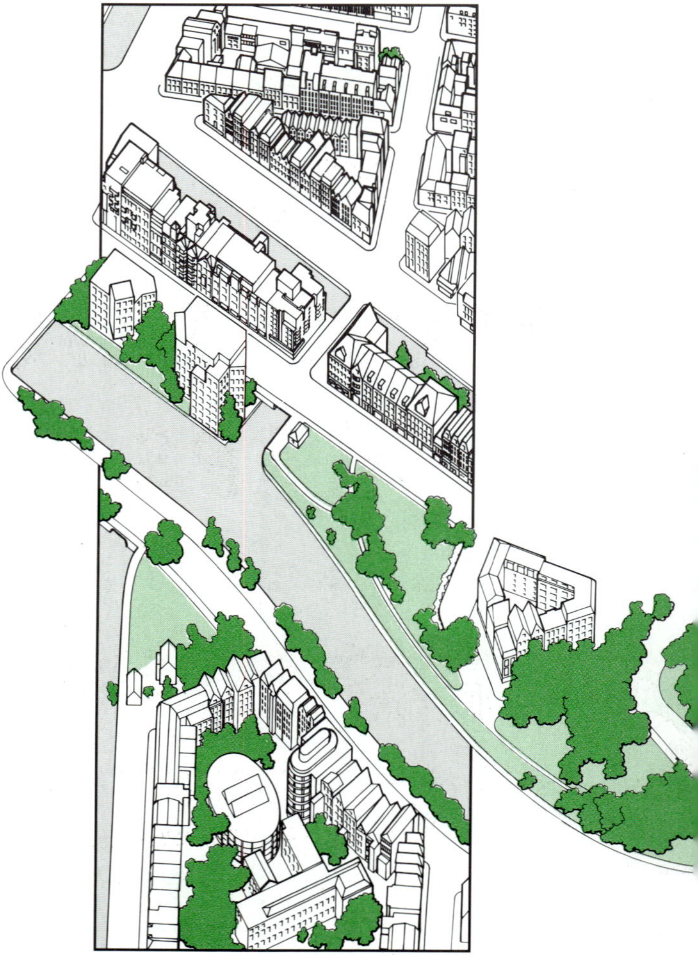

The Isometric Maps

LE MAIREGRACHT
VAN NOORDTKADE
VAN NOORDTGRACHT
HOUTMANKADE
WESTER KANAAL
DIRK HARTOGHSTRAAT
VAN HEEMSKERCKSTRAAT
HOUTMANKADE
VAN LINSCHOTENSTRAAT
ROGGEVEENS
1
BARENTSZSTRAAT
ZOUTKEETSPLEIN
ZOUTKEETSGRACHT
ZOUTKEETSGRACHT
2
ZOUTKEETS-GRACHT
HOUTMANSTRAAT
HOUTMAN-DWARSSTR.
7
HOUTMANKADE
SMALLE PADS GRACHT
VIERWINDENSTR
VIERWINDEN-DWARSSTRAAT
REALENGRAC
PLANCIUSSTRAAT
2e BREEUWERSSTRAAT
1e BREEUWERSSTRAAT
NIEUWE TEERTUINEN
PRINSENEILANDSGRACHT
PRINSENEILAND
6
SLOTERDIJKSTRAAT
GALGENSTRAAT
PRINSENEILAND

▼ 38

Western Islands (Westelijke Eilanden)

To the northwest of Centraal Station lies the Westerdok (Western Dock) and the islands of Prinseneiland, Bickerseiland and Realeneiland, well worth a visit for anyone with more than a few days to spend in Amsterdam. Cut off to the east by the harbour and to the south by the railway tracks, the area was once devoted to shipping, populated by boatmen and infiltrated only by artists, and has a remote, bracing quality. In recent years, large-scale development has taken place, and modern housing blocks, converted warehouses, peaceful canals, white wooden drawbridges, barges, yachts and ferries coexist in harmony. ① **Joseph Lam Jazzclub** (8 Van Diemenstraat), atmospheric trad and Dixieland jazz club, Fri-Sun. ② **Zoutkeetsgracht**, where a mixture of new housing developments and well-worn boatyards typify the area. ③ **Zandhoek**, quiet, cobbled and framed by white drawbridges. **Nos 2-7** are a late 17thC group of dramatic black and white houses whose front doors are set into a huge expanse of windows spanning two floors. Opposite is a line of splendid gleaming old barges. **Nos 8-15** are also attractive. ④ No. 14 is the restaurant **De Gouden Reael**, a most welcome find. In an airy, split-level conversion, the restaurant is on the first floor, with a bar downstairs. The cooking is French provincial, with a new region introduced every three months: the young chef shows knowledge of her subject and a light touch (**fff**). In summer the barge opposite makes an agreeable outdoor terrace on which to lunch, dine or merely drink. ⑤ Along Bickersgracht a **children's farm** adds to the rural flavour. ⑥ On **Prinseneiland**, old shuttered warehouses, many converted, and little shipyards recall another age. ⑦ If you are walking this way (through fairly dismal surroundings), pop round the corner into **Houtmanstraat**, a tree-lined street of mid-l9thC philanthropic housing for the poor. The highly developed Dutch sense of social responsibility crops up everywhere in Amsterdam. To the west of the Westerkanaal are some important buildings of the famous Amsterdam School (1910-30), when urban architecture attained the highest standards (off map). Enthusiasts will wish to view Michel de Klerk's **Eigen Haard** housing project on Spaarndammerplantsoen, his **Postkantoor** (post office) on Zaanstraat and his housing block on Hembrugstraat, with its purposeless, yet symbolic and unifying tower.

▲ 36

5
HAARLEMMERPLEIN
KORTE MARNIX KADE
SINGELGRACHT
KORTE MARNIXSTRAAT
KORTE WAGENSTR.
NIEUWE WAGENSTRAAT
EILANDSGRACHT
HAARLEMMER HOUTTUINEN
NIEUWE HOUTTUINEN
BUITEN DOMMERSSTR.
BAANBRUGSTEEG
VINKENSTRAAT
MARNIXSTRAAT
BROUWERSGRACHT
BINNEN DOMMERSSTRAAT
MOUTHAANSTEEG
LIJNBAANSGRACHT
DRIEHOEKSTRAAT
KROMME PALMSTR.
3
1
BROUWERSGRACHT
PALMGRACHT
LIJNBAANSGRACHT
PALMSTRAAT
PALMDWARSSTRAAT
WILLEMSSTRAAT
1e GOUDSBLOEMDWARSSTRAAT
2e GOUDSBLOEMDWARSSTR.
GOUDSBLOEMSTRAAT

▼ 40

Brouwersgracht

① The jolly, happy-go-lucky feel of the **Brouwersgracht** makes a pleasant contrast to the unrelenting elegance of the great Grachtengordel (Canal Ring). On the edge of the Jordaan (*see pages 41, 69*), the `brewers' canal' was built for work, not for living. Today of course, apartments have mostly replaced stacks of ships' cargo in the warehouses, and houseboats (one with a greenhouse on its roof) line the canal, which is spanned by cast-iron drawbridges. At No. 202 a brick and beamed warehouse cellar has become the **Spitsbergen** wine shop. ② The wide junction with **Prinsengracht**, outermost, humblest and most informal of the three great canals, affords pleasant open views in all directions (except for the trains): old houses, trees, canals clogged with houseboats. ③ One of several 17thC almshouses (*hofjes*) to be found in the Jordaan, each one a little courtyard of dwellings hiding behind the street door - peek in and see. This one, **Rapenhofje** (Nos 28-38), is particularly charming. It was built in 1648 by Pieter Adriaensz Raep, whose surname means turnip, hence the carved turnip above the door. Close by is **Bosschehofje** at Nos 20-26. ④ Across the Brouwersgracht the atmosphere changes. This is a close-knit community centred on **Haarlemmerdijk** and its continuation, Haarlemmerstraat (*see page 42*), a bustling local shopping street with food and hardware shops, cafés, restaurants and the odd idiosyncratic little clothing or craft shop. Notable is the Dutch cheese shop on the corner of Prinsengracht. ⑤ **Haarlemmerpoort**, undistinguished former city gate, now converted into apartments.

▲ 38

GOUDSBLOEMSTRAAT
2e GOUDSBLOEMDWARSSTR.
1e GOUDSBLOEMDWARSSTRAAT
3e GOUDSBLOEM-DWARSSTR.
LINDENGRACHT
1
1e LINDENDWARSSTRAAT
2e LINDENDWARSSTRAAT
LINDENSTRAAT
KARTHUIZERSDWARSSTRAAT
KARTHUIZERSPLANTSOEN
KARTHUIZERSSTRAAT
1e BOOMDWARSSTRAAT
BOOMSTRAAT
2e BOOMDWARSSTRAAT
9
TICHELSTRAAT
WESTERSTRAAT
VIOLETTENSTRAAT
10
1e ANJELIERSDWARSSTR.
ANJELIERSSTRAAT
2e ANJELIERSDWARSSTR.
12
1e TUINDWARSSTR.
13
2e TUINDWARSSTR.
TUINSTRAAT
14
1e EGELANTIERSDWARSSTR.
PRINSENGRACHT
EGELANTIERSSTRAAT
2e EGELANTIERSDWARSSTR.
15
16
EGELANTIERSGRACHT

▼ 48

The Jordaan

Outside the Grachtengordel (Canal Ring), but also dating from the 17thC, the Jordaan was developed as an industrial working-class area. Over the years it has become the adopted home of refugees, artists and students. Its dense grid of narrow streets buzzes with life. ① Peek into the **Suyckerhofje** (1670), one of the many almshouses, with its lush wilderness of a garden. Another feature of the area is the gablestone: a tile set into the façade of a house, indicating the inhabitant's occupation, or a joke; for example, the 'Topsy-turvy World' on ② **Nos 55-7**, where fish live in a tree and the date is upside down. Perfect places to sip a *jenever* and read the Sunday papers, the brown cafés ③ **Papeneiland**, with its Delft-tiled wall, and newer but equally charming ④ **'t Smackzeyl**. ⑤ **Noordermarkt**. On Monday you will find everything from brocade to fake fur at the textile market, and an array of junk at the flea market. Saturday sees a bird market and the *Boerenmarkt*, which sells organic food. In the square, **Woutertje Pieterse** (No. 4) is an excellent coffee shop; **Bordewijk** (No. 7), a chic restaurant with an innovative French-based menu (**ff**); and No. 34, a lovingly preserved brown café, **J.A. Hegeraad**. ⑥ Now sadly dilapidated, Hendrick de Keyser's swansong, **Noorderkerk** was a pioneer of design in 1620, an austere octagonal brick church, with four hipped roofs. ⑦ 19thC **Hofje De Star**, grand but functional. ⑧ **Zon's Hofje** has a hushed verdant courtyard. ⑨ **Huiszitten-Weduwenhof**, early housing for poor widows by Daniel Stalpaert. ⑩ Food, clothes and electrical goods are available at **Westerstraat**'s general Monday market. ⑪ A pink confection, the free-standing 19thC facade is all that remains of the original building at **151 Prinsengracht**, Louise-Bewaar-school. ⑫ Beautifully restored **Claes Claesz Hofje** (1616), now occupied by students of the Conservatory of Music and the Academy of Fine Arts; it incorporates pretty **Anslo's Hofje**, with its hotch-potch of tiny houses. ⑬ **Jurriaans**, genial café with. ⑭ Squeeze through the crowd into **Café 't Smalle**, an exquisite ivy-clad brown café, with panels, beams and stained glass windows. ⑮ Good cabaret and international cuisine at **De Kikker** (**ff**). ⑯ Pieter de Keyser's **Huis met de Hoofden** (House with the Heads), in extravagant Dutch Renaissance style, with a balustraded step gable and pilasters bearing the heads of classical gods.

▲ 41

BUITEN BROUWERSSTRAAT
HAARLEMMER HOUTTUIN
KORTE PRINSENGRACHT
HAARLEMMERSTRAAT
BUITEN WIERINGERS
BINNEN BROUWERSSTRAAT
HERENMARKT
HERENMARKT
BINNEN WIERINGERSTRAAT
BINNEN VISSERS
BROUWERSGRACHT
BROUWERSGRACHT
BROUWERS
KEIZERSGRACHT
KEIZERSGRACHT
KEIZERSGRACHT
ROOMOLENSTRAAT
HERENGRACHT
HERENGRACHT
HERENGRACHT
LANGESTRAAT
SING
KORSJESPOORTSTEEG
TEER
HERENSTRAAT
SINGEL
KORSJESPOORTST
KORTE
BLAUWBURGWAL
BLAUWBURGWAL
OUDE NIEUWSTRAAT
1
3
5
6
7
12
16
17
18

▼ 50

Grachtengordel/Brouwersgracht

To cope with the 17thC population explosion, the city carpenter Hendrick Staets devised the elegant Grachtengordel, ring of three canals, which begin here and stretch to the Amstel. ① **Café du Lac**, chic café decked out like a church. ② Aesthetically pleasing despite its grimy exterior, **Schipperskinderenschool** (1925). ③ **Westindisch Huis** (1615), where the city of New York had its conception, and the Lutheran Orphanage was housed in the 19thC. Its elegant classical proportions are offset by a flamboyant pediment sculpture of a swan. ④ A blue angel surveys the scene from his perch at the top of the lofty 19thC **Spaanse Huis** (Spanish House). ⑤ Opulent mansions line the grand canal the merchants built for themselves, the **Herengracht** (Gentlemen's Canal). ⑥ The gay, fashionable **Hotel New York** in three 17thC canal houses (**ff**). ⑦ Smaller, less sumptuous houses characterize the **Keizersgracht** (Emperor's Canal). ⑧ The original city moat, the **Singel** marks the transition between medieval and 17thC Amsterdam. ⑨ Reputedly the smallest house in Amsterdam, **No. 7** is in fact the doorway to the flats next door. ⑩ Past an alluring parade of antique shops, the luxury modern **Sonesta Hotel** (**fff**) pampers its guests not only with five-star comfort, but also an excellent American regional restaurant (**ff**), a disco and well-equipped fitness centre. Receptions and Sunday morning concerts are held in ⑪ the deconsecrated **Ronde Lutherse Kerk**. Adriaen Dortsman's original 17thC church burnt down in 1822, was rebuilt in the same classical style, and its fine verdigris copper dome remains the most impressive sight on the Singel. ⑫ Dating back to the Herengracht's earliest days are the spout-gabled warehouses **De Fortuyn** and **d'Arcke Noach** (c1600). ⑬ Chintzy little **Singel Hotel** (**ff**). ⑭ The city's oldest restaurant, **De Silveren Spiegel** inhabits a wonderfully quaint step-gabled house, with tiny-paned windows, which leans precariously. It has an unpretentious French-inspired menu and excellent wine list (**ff**). ⑮ **Holiday Inn Crowne Plaza** (**fff**), deluxe hotel, with a pleasant restaurant, **The Seven Seas** (**fff**). ⑯ Hundreds of feline waifs and strays are given refuge in **De Poezenboot** (The Cat Boat). ⑰ The different types of gable, which evolved as the Herengracht was built, are evident in **Nos 79-87**. ⑱ '50s-style **De Beiaard** boasts a huge selection of draught beers.

44

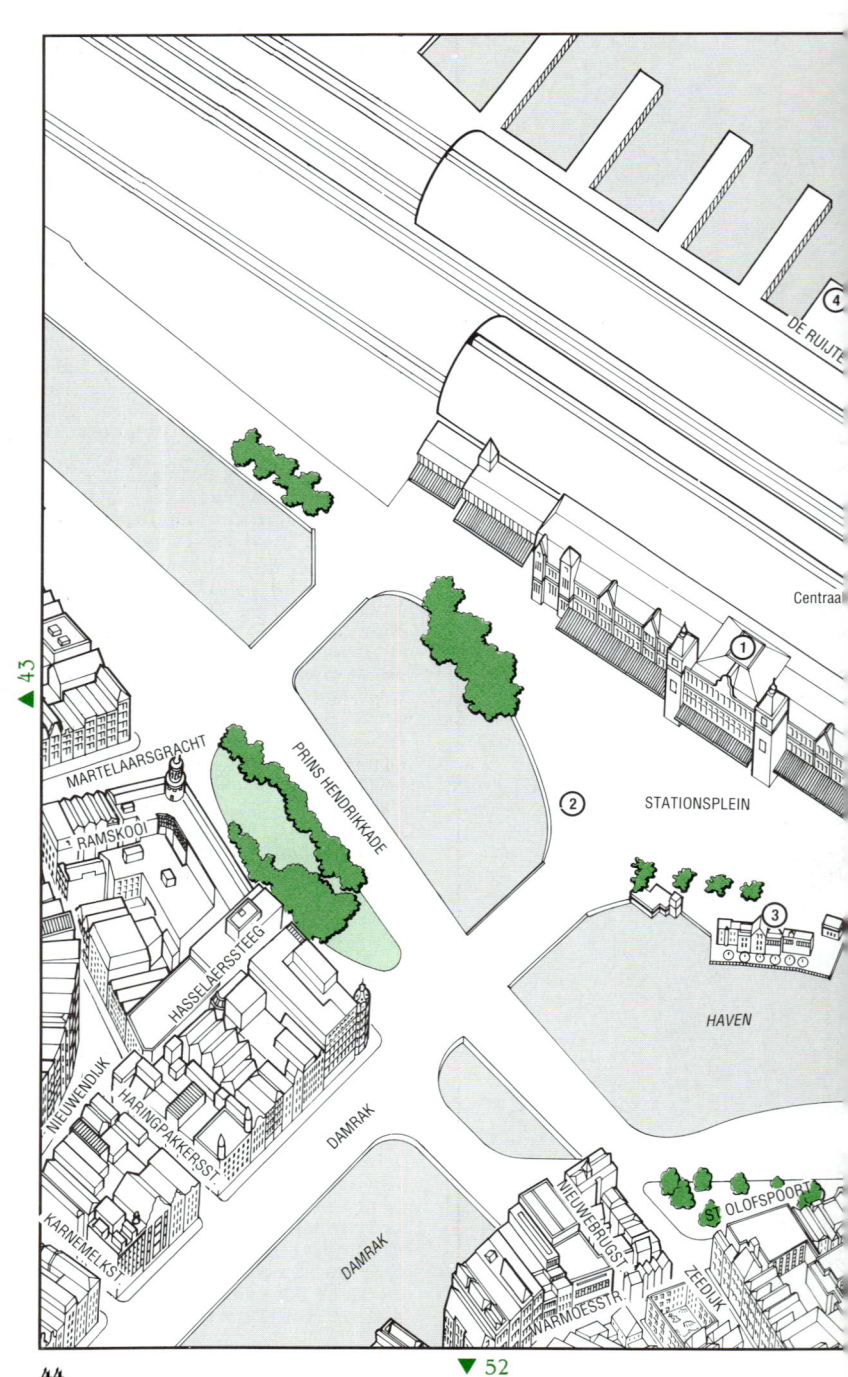

▲ 43

▼ 52

- ④ DE RUIJTE
- Centraal
- ①
- ② STATIONSPLEIN
- ③
- ⑤ OLOFSPOORT
- MARTELAARSGRACHT
- RAMSKOOI
- PRINS HENDRIKKADE
- HASSELAERSSTEEG
- NIEUWENDIJK
- HARINGPAKKERSS.
- KARNEMELKST.
- DAMRAK
- NIEUWEBRUGST.
- DAMRAK
- ZEEDIJK
- WARMOESSTR.
- HAVEN

Centraal Station

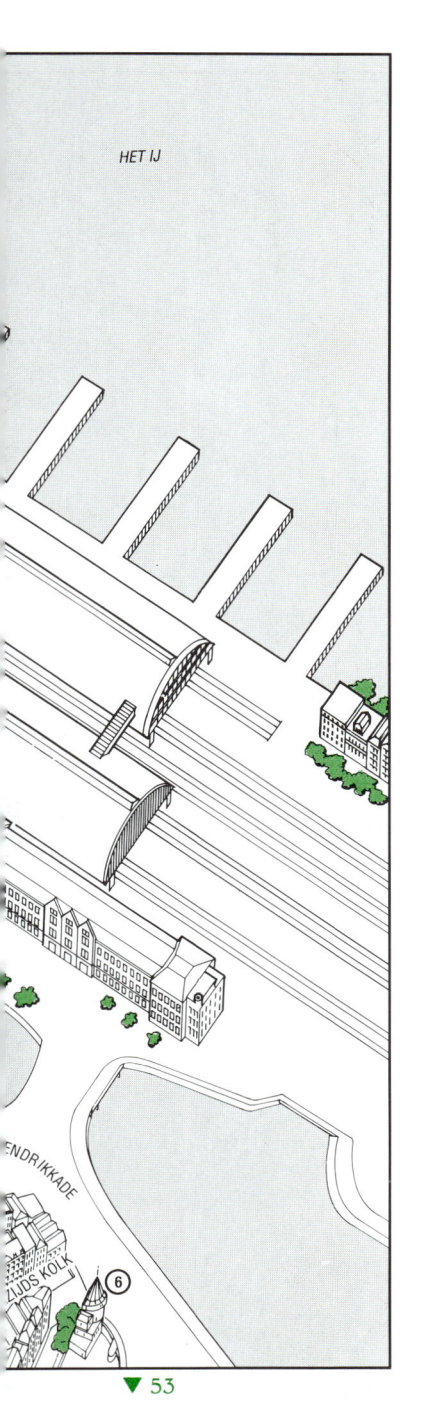

For many visitors, Amsterdam begins at Centraal Station. Where, you might wonder, as you plunge through Stationsplein and into Damrak, is the city's famous stately beauty? Yet what this key area lacks in charm, it gains in liveliness, and your day will kick off to a brisk start. ① **Centraal Station** was built in the 1880s by neo-Gothic architect P.J.H. Cuypers, who was also responsible for the startlingly similar Rijksmuseum and was influenced by Frenchman Viollet-le-Duc. The fact that the building blocked Amsterdammers' view of the port and open sea caused much controversy at the time. The ornate façade depicts themes of travel, trade and city history. Here, and in ② **Stationsplein** outside, you will find a 24-hour bureau de change, left luggage facilities, including bikes, a **VVV** tourist information centre, public transport information, and trams departing for all corners of the city. If you have time to while away, choose from turn-of-the-century splendour at the former first-class waiting room, **Grand Café le Klas** (near track 2b; **ff**) or the waterside terrace of ③ the **Noord-Zuid Hollandsch Koffiehuis** (**f**) in the same wooden pavilion, restored in 1982 after the building of the metro, as the VVV. ④ An amusing, salty and free ride can be had from here on the **ferry** across the River IJ to the suburb of Amsterdam North, a part of the city which is the subject of exciting new development. (There are also major development plans for the disused Eastern Docks near the station.) ⑤ **St Nicolaaskerk**, Catholic church built in 1887 after Catholicism was again allowed to flourish (*see Amstelkring Museum page 53*). ⑥ The medieval **Schreierstoren**, defensive tower of an early city wall. Folklore says that from here weeping women waved farewell to their seafaring men as recorded by a 16thC tablet. A 20thC plaque commemorates the departure of Henry Hudson for America in 1609. Nearby, towards the station, notice at **No. 85, Gebouw Batavia**, the terracotta sculptures which recall the city's colonial past.

1e HUGO DE GROOTSTRAAT
MARNIXKADE
EGELANTIERSSTRAAT
NIEUWE EGELANTIERSSTR.
WESTERKADE
NASSAUKADE
EGELANTIERSGRACHT
3e LELIEDWARSSTRAAT
MARNIXSTRAAT
LIJNBAANSGRACHT
2e MARNIX-PLANTSOEN
BLOEMGRACHT
SINGELGRACHT
8
9
10
12
13
AKOLEIENSTRAAT
LIJNBAANSGRACHT
2e ROZENDWARSSTR.

▼ 56

Jordaan/Rozengracht

Primarily a working-class district, dotted with workshops, garages and housing developments. ① Pretty and private, the courtyard of the small-scale **St Andrieshofje**. It was built in 1616 with the fortune left by cattle farmer Ivo Gerritszoon, and is one of the city's oldest almshouses. ② An inviting if eccentric row of shops includes **Al Maghreb**, selling North African pottery (No. 9); a retro clothes boutique, **Bop Street** (No. 7); **Electric Lady**, a kitsch art shop; and **De Vliegende Kikker** for painted wooden animals (No. 3). ③ A favourite Indonesian restaurant is **Speciaal** (f), where wicker chairs, bamboo-clad walls and authentic Indonesian cooking trick the mind into believing this is Java rather than Amsterdam. It takes courage to order the fiery *rijsttafel*. ④ **De Nieuwe Lelie**, congenial modern brown café on two levels, with its own café cat. ⑤ **De Groene Lantaarn**, cosy fondue restaurant in an old carriage house, with a remarkable choice of ingredients, including fish (**ff**). ⑥ **Bloemgracht**, tagged the 'Herengracht of the Jordaan', because of its elaborate gables. ⑦ Steep step gables grace **Nos 87-91**, three identical dollshouses of 1642, their tiny green-paned leaded windows protected by distinctive black and red shutters. The three gablestones portray three men of the city, country and sea. ⑧ An illustration of unorthodox 19thC municipal architecture, B. de Greef's **Politiebureau Raampoort** (1888). ⑨ Although a tumbledown house is a common sight in Amsterdam, **164 Bloemstraat** is one of the worst, supported entirely by sturdy wooden posts. ⑩ **Fons Welters**, contemporary sculpture gallery. ⑪ Set back from the shabby Rozengracht by a little courtyard, in a pretty step-gabled house is **Bols Taveerne**, the former distillery of the Bols family. The restaurant has several attractive rooms with antique furniture and marine paintings. The cuisine is French with hints of Italian, and fish dominates a changing menu. The management will arrange for guests to be collected and returned in one of their chauffeur-driven cars (**ff**). ⑫ **Eben Haezer**, recommended youth hostel. ⑬ A plaque marks the site of **No. 184**, the house where Rembrandt lived the last years of his life in poverty.

▲ 40

EGELANTIERSGR.
EGELANTIERSGRACHT
NIEUWE LELIESTRAAT
1e LELIEDWARSSTRAAT
PRINSENGRACHT
LELIEGRACHT
KEIZERSGRACHT
BLOEMGRACHT
BLOEMGRACHT
KEIZERSGRACHT
BLOEMSTR
WESTERMARKT
RAADHUISSTRAAT
ROZENGRACHT
PRINSENGRACHT
ROZENSTR
PRINSENGRACHT
KEIZERSGRACHT
LAURIERSTR
REESTRAAT
HARTENSTRAAT
LAURIERGR.
1
2
3
4
5
6
7
8
9
10
11
12
13
14
15
16
17

▲ 47

▼ 58

Grachtengordel/Raadhuisstraat

① Famous brown café, **De Twee Zwaantjes**, with live accordion music that ranges from music hall to opera. ② **Christophe'** (pronounced `Christoph Apostroph'), not only one of the trendiest places to be seen in, but the worthy possessor of a Michelin star (ff). ③ An example of the rare **bottle gable**, aptly above a bar. ④ A pretty stretch of the **Leliegracht**; note **No. 25**, its windows crowned with scallop shells. ⑤ You can't miss van Arkel's imposing art nouveau building at **263 Keizersgracht**. ⑥ The harrowing story of a young Jewish girl and her family is brought to life in **Anne Frank Huis**, a typical 17thC canal house, with an annexe, where the Franks and four friends hid for over two years from the Nazis, until betrayed and sent to concentration camps. Anne described their captivity in her poignant diary. The stark interior has no furniture, but is otherwise as it was: the hinged bookcase concealing the annexe; Anne's pin-ups of movie stars; pencil markings recording the girls' heights. A display about Anne and her diary and temporary exhibitions relating to the Anne Frank Foundation are downstairs. ⑦ **Rum Runners**, bustling restaurant, where tropical décor and live music set the mood for Caribbean cuisine (ff). ⑧ A statue of Anne Frank stands outside Hendrick de Keyser's Renaissance-style **Westerkerk** (1620-31), its tiered spire, topped by the yellow and blue imperial crown. Between the buttresses tiny shops sell jewellery, china and glass. ⑨ In a 1638 house by Philips Vingboons, sporting the city's first neck gable and with a sumptuous 18thC Louis XIV-style interior, **Nederlands Theater Museum** has a colourful display of models, machinery, props, costumes and stage sets. ⑩ **Rinascimento, Galleria d'Arte**, a seductive little shop, crammed with antique and modern Delftware as well as colourful Italian Majolica. ⑪ **Bartolotti House**, built by de Keyser in 1617, with a glorious step gable piled high with urns, and a dashing red brick and white stone facade, curving with the canal. ⑫ Combining 20thC chic with old beams and bare bricks, **Pulitzer Hotel** was created from a series of canal houses (fff). Explore the enticing shops along ⑬ **Reestraat** and ⑭ **Hartenstraat** such as ⑮ **Terra**, for beautiful continental pottery and terracotta urns; and ⑯ **Varenkamp**, where the owner sells his own bold and amusing paintings and pottery. ⑰ **Van Harte**, stylish restaurant with a Provençal flavour (ff).

▲ 42

▲ 49

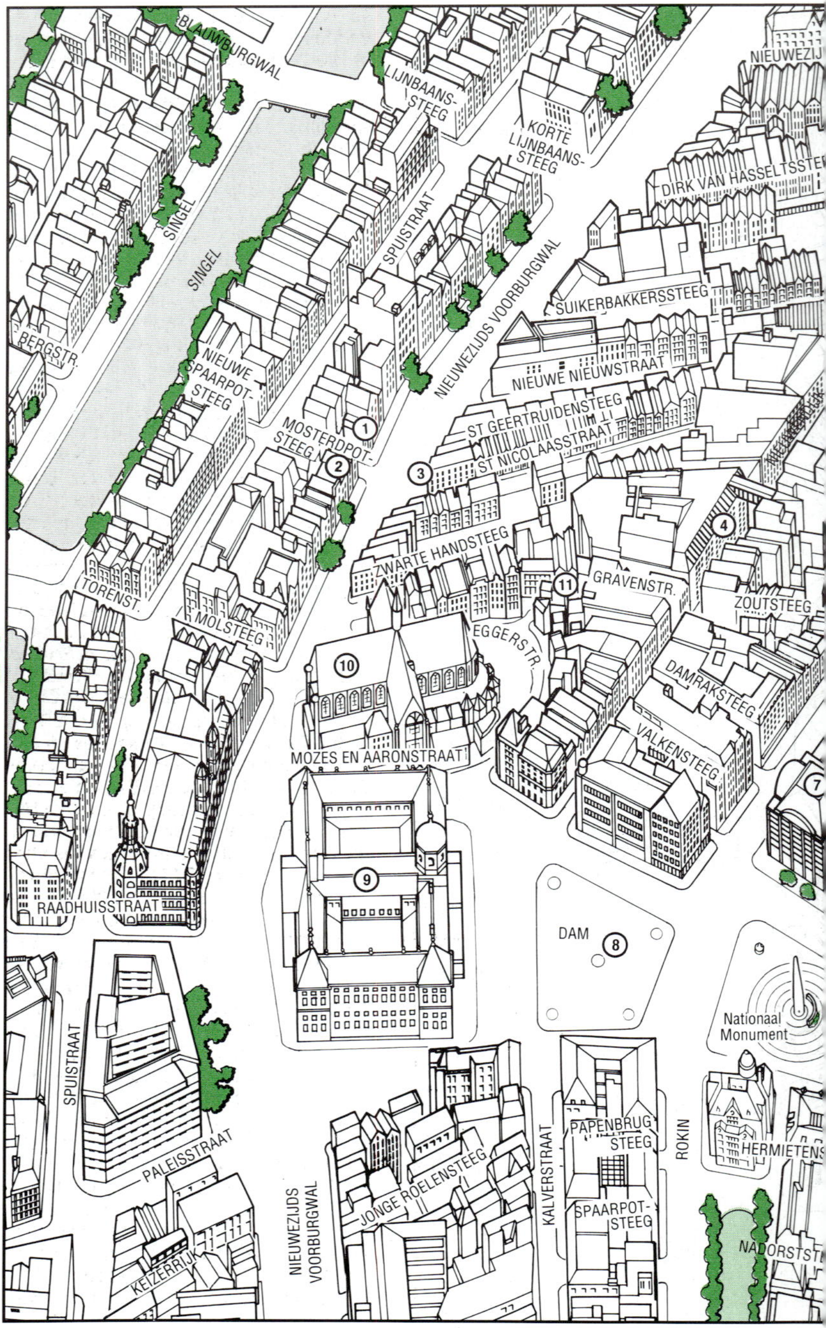
BLAUWBURGWAL
LIJNBAANS-STEEG
KORTE LIJNBAANS-STEEG
NIEUWEZIJ
DIRK VAN HASSELTSSTE
SINGEL
SINGEL
SPUISTRAAT
NIEUWEZIJDS VOORBURGWAL
SUIKERBAKKERSSTEEG
BERGSTR.
NIEUWE SPAARPOT-STEEG
NIEUWE NIEUWSTRAAT
MOSTERDPOT-STEEG
1
2
3
ST GEERTRUIDENSTEEG
ST NICOLAASSTRAAT
4
ZWARTE HANDSTEEG
11
GRAVENSTR.
ZOUTSTEEG
TORENST.
MOLSTEEG
10
EGGERSTR.
DAMRAKSTEEG
VALKENSTEEG
MOZES EN AARONSTRAAT
7
9
RAADHUISSTRAAT
DAM
8
Nationaal Monument
SPUISTRAAT
PALEISSTRAAT
NIEUWEZIJDS VOORBURGWAL
JONGE ROELENSTEEG
KALVERSTRAAT
PAPENBRUG STEEG
ROKIN
HERMIETENS
SPAARPOT-STEEG
NADORSTST
KEIZERRIJK

▼ 60

Dam Square

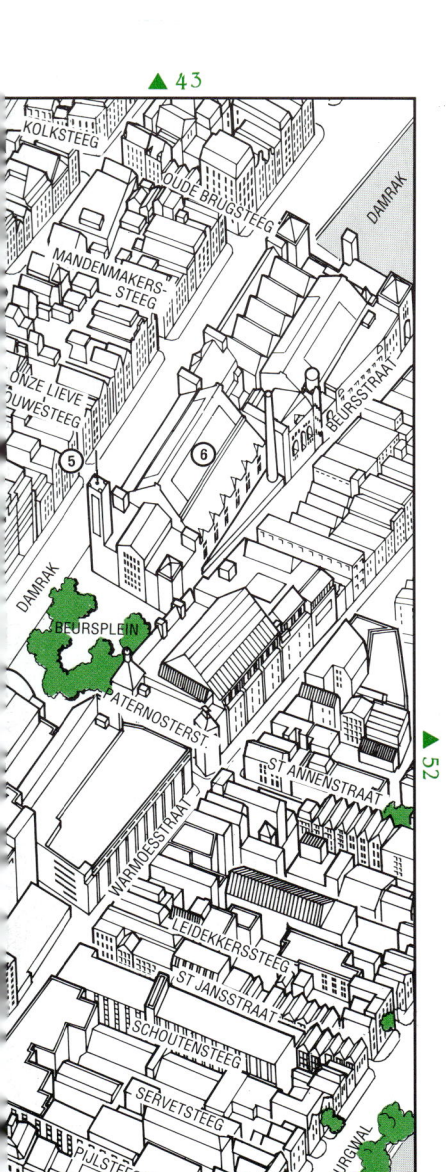

As your tram rattles down the Nieuwezijds Voorburgwal, notice ① the yellow awnings of **Die Port van Cleve** (ff), famed since 1870 for its pea soup and steak, and ② the ostentatious **Post Office** (1899), now a shopping mall. ③ **Treasure** (ff), a good Chinese. ④ **Nieuwendijk** is an unappetising pedestrian shopping street. ⑤ In the 1930s **Allert de Lange** published the work of refugees from Nazi Germany such as Brecht and Brod. Today it is a bookshop strong on travel, art and literature in English, French, German and Dutch. ⑥ The innovative **Beurs** (Stock Exchange) **van Berlage** was derided when it was unveiled in 1903, but is now universally admired. The work of the pioneer of Dutch modern architecture, H.P. Berlage, it is used for concerts and exhibitions. Try to see the exceptionally light and spacious interior. The current Beurs (1913) is adjacent. ⑦ **De Bijenkorf**, the city's top department store, but still pretty run-of-the-mill. ⑧ **Dam Square** is both the start and the heart of Amsterdam. Here was the original 13thC dam on the river Amstel around which a small fishing community grew into a great city. The **Nationaal Monument** commemorating World War II attracts a motley crowd of pushers, tourists and hangers-on; **Madame Tussaud Scenerama** is located in the upper floors of Peek and Cloppenburg; the **Grand Hotel Krasnapolsky** (fff) was founded in 1883 by a Polish emigré. Over all looms the bulk of ⑨ the **Koninklijk Paleis**. Built as the town hall, and supported by 13,659 wooden piles, Jacob van Campen's unsmiling classical edifice symbolizes the civic pride and power of 17thC Amsterdam. Both the exterior and the startlingly magnificent interior are embellished by the work of Antwerp sculptor Artus Quellinus the Elder. Town hall was promoted to Royal Palace by Louis Bonaparte, Napoleon's brother who crowned himself King of the Netherlands in 1806, and bequeathed the handsome Empire furniture. The present Royal Family live elsewhere, and the exterior looks unkempt and forlorn. ⑩ **Nieuwe Kerk** is the setting for royal coronations (Queen Beatrix's was in 1980). It was built in late Gothic style in the 15thC, and reconstructed several times after fires. It is now a social and cultural centre. ⑪ Pop into **Gravenstraat** to visit the tiny shops built amongst the buttresses of the church, and the ancient *proeflokaal* (tasting house), **De Drie Fleschjes**.

▲ 44

DAMRAK
DAMRAK
NIEUWEBRUGST.
ZEEDIJK
OUDEZIJDS KOL
ELLEBO
WIJNGAARDSSTRAATJE
OUDEZIJDS ARMSTEEG
OUDEBRUGSTEEG
WARMOESSTRAAT
BEURSSTRAAT
HEINTJE HOEKSTEEG
VREDEN-BURGERST.
SPOOKSTE
LANGE NIEZEL
ENGE KERKSTEEG
KORTE NIEZEL
ZEEDIJK
STORMSTEEG
WIJDE KERKSTEEG
OUDEZIJDS VORBURGWAL
OUDEZIJDS ACHTERBURGWAL
BOOMSTEEG
OUDEKERKSPLEIN
ST ANNEN DWARSSTRAAT
OUDEKENNISSTEEG
ST ANNENSTRAAT
OUDEZIJDS VOORBURGWAL
MOLENSTEEG
KREUPELST.
MONNIKENSTRAAT
OUDEZIJDS ACHTERBURGWAL
BLOEDSTRAAT
NIEUWMARKT
STOOFSTEEG
BARNDESTEEG
KOESTRAAT
BETHANIENSTRAAT
KLOVENIERSBURGWAL
KLOVENIERSBURGWAL
ST ANTONIESBREESTRAAT
1
2
3
4
5
6
7
8
9
10
11
12
13
14

▲ 51

▼ 62

De Walletjes (Red Light District)

The oldest profession in the world aptly occupies Amsterdam's oldest quarter, and its origins are bound up with the city's own as a port. With the influx of foreigners, prostitution flourished, and today, though illegal, it is tolerated. ① A rare medieval wooden house, **No. 1 Zeedijk** stands at the head of an infamous street, where few but drug-dealers, junkies and the police venture. A clean-up programme is under way, but opinion is split as to its effectiveness. ② The city's oldest street, **Warmoesstraat**, 'delicatessen street', has run to seed. Restaurants, cafés and delis jostle for space with gay nightclubs, leather bars and speciality shops, such as the offbeat **Condomerie Het Gulden Vlies** at No. 141, which stocks condoms of all shapes and sizes in a serious attempt to promote health. ③ **Hotel Kabul**, cheap and cheerful single, double and triple rooms, plus dormitories for up to ten (**f**). ④ Along **Oudezijds Voorburgwal**, prostitutes, old and young, pouting or indifferent, scantily clad in black lace or satin, sit in windows or loll in doorways. In among the sex shows and porno shops is some interesting 17thC architecture: **Nos 14, 22** and **57**. ⑤ **Museum Amstelkring** or "Our Lord in the Attic" is a gem, the sole survivor of scores of clandestine churches built after the Alteration of 1578 outlawed open Catholicism. Exploring its perfectly preserved rooms is like stepping into a Vermeer. The delightful galleried attic church was created by rich merchant Jan Hartman in 1660. ⑥ **Centra**, no-frills restaurant, serving the best Spanish cuisine in town (**f**). ⑦ A heavenly jumble of architectural styles, from medieval to Renaissance, **Oude Kerk** boasts beautiful timber roofs and misericords, among other treasures. ⑧ The aroma of coffee beans will lure you into **Wijs & Zonen**, a charming old-fashioned coffee shop. ⑨ **Bulldog**, first of the so-called 'hash coffee shops', where you can buy and smoke a joint with your *cappuccino*, or with a cocktail at the No. 132 branch. ⑩ Heart of the diminutive **Chinatown**. ⑪ **Nieuw-markt**, scene of a Sunday antique market in summer. ⑫ Bulky 15thC **Waag**, the eastern gate in the city's defences. In the 17thC, it became a weighing-house and home to numerous guilds, including the surgeons', and it was here that Rembrandt painted his famous *Anatomy Lesson of Dr Tulp*. ⑬ **The Shelter** youth hostel. ⑭ Identical neck gables, **Abraham and Isaac**, bearing reliefs of father and son.

OOSTERDOKSKADE

BUITEN BANTAMMERSTRAAT

PRINS HENDRIKKADE

BINNENKANT

SCHIPPERSSTRAAT

WAALSEILANDSGRACHT

NIEUWE JONKERSTR.

OUDE WAAL

MONTELBAANSTRAAT

NIEUWE RIDDERSTRAAT

RECHT BOOMSSLOOT

OUDESCHANS

KALKMARKT

'S GRAVENHEKJE

RAPENBURG

OUDESCHANS

▲ 53

▼ 64

54

Oosterdok

The docks are still steeped in the spirit of Amsterdam's great maritime past. Van Gogh described the appeal of their "... old, narrow and rather sombre streets, with their shops occupied by chemists, lithographers and ships' chandlers...." ① One 20thC landmark is **Stationspost-gebouw** (1968), a long low district post office building, inspired by Le Corbusier. ② Among the city's most improbable sights, **Sea Palace Restaurant** in a float-ing pagoda. A small-scale replica of a restaurant in Hong Kong Harbour, it still manages to pack in 800 for an agreeable Chinese dinner (**f**). ③ Built between 1911 and 1916 as offices for a clutch of shipping companies by Johan van der Mey, Michel de Klerk and P.L. Kramer, the fanciful **Scheepvaarthuis** gave birth to the Amsterdam School of architecture. This monumental dark brick building is smothered in nautical visual whimsy - expressionistic monsters, mariners and mermaids. A 20thC fortress, with strong vertical lines and turrets, it now houses the Municipal Transport Authority. ④ **No. 131 Prins Hendrikkade**, home of Admiral de Ruyter, who sailed up the Medway River in 1667 and set the English fleet on fire. ⑤ **Buiten Bantammerstraat**, a welcome little green oasis off the busy thoroughfare. ⑥ Bordering Waalseilandsgracht, an attractive side canal dotted with houseboats, **Binnenkant** is lined with fine old houses, once the homes of wealthy merchants, keen to advertise their seafaring connections: for instance ⑦ the gablestone of a fishing boat that bears the date 1592. Towering over ⑧ the now lovely **Oude Schans**, site of the first shipyards, which later deteriorated into a seedy outpost of the Jewish Quarter, ⑨ **Montelbaanstoren** is a fortified tower, built in 1512 to defend the Dutch fleet. The openwork steeple was added by the ubiquitous Hendrick de Keyser in 1606, when the city fathers felt that they could at last afford the icing on the cake. ⑩ The striking building at **No. 1 's Gravenhekje** (1642) is a group of four warehouses that belonged to the Dutch West India Company and later became their HQ. Two identical trapezium-shaped gables span its width, with an ornate pediment, bearing the company's coat of arms.

▲ 46

Lijnbaansgracht/Jordaan

The only reason to visit this dull stretch of Lijnbaansgracht is ① **Robert & Abraham Kef**, an engagingly old-fashioned wood-furnished shoe box of a shop, where you can sample delectable cheeses, imported from all over France: Port-Salut, Vacherin, Bresse Bleu, Fourme d'Ambert and many more. It also sells French wine, bread, pâté and other delicacies. To the east, in the liveliest quarter of the Jordaan, ② **Rooie Nelis** is a traditional neon-lit working men's café. ③ The ground floor of a pretty ivy-clad corner house is occupied by the anachronistic second-hand clothes boutique, **Sisters**, which sells exclusively 1960s and 1970s fashions, from silver platform shoes to tie-dyed T-shirts and psychedelic mini-skirts. ④ **Steendrukkerij Amsterdam**, gallery dealing in prints, lithographs and woodcuts. ⑤ **The English Bookshop** sells English and American magazines as well as books. ⑥ In the heart of the Jordaan, **Hazenstraat** is lined with trendy boutiques selling distinctive off-beat clothes. Among the most eye-catching, ⑦ **'t Haasje** specializes in Oriental-style gilt-embroidered clothes for women, in beautiful rich colours. ⑧ Men are strictly excluded from **Vrouwen Café Saarein**, a cosy brown café where women can chat, drink and play darts or billiards. The staff will supply information on women's activities in the city. ⑨ **Car park**. ⑩ A bustling homely little restaurant, its walls crammed with prints and photos, **Het Stuivertje** boasts a tempting French menu that changes every fortnight. The food is not only superb, but also excellent value (**f**). ⑪ **Baobab**, a treasure trove of Oriental knick-nacks, ornaments and jewellery, although you can also unearth carpets, tables, trays and bags. ⑫ **Antiekmarkt De Looier**. In a confusing warren of tiny alleyways, scruffy stalls sell almost anything from rickety chairs and rusty farm implements to some genuinely good jewellery and furniture. ⑬ **Police station**. ⑭ On the pretty, quiet **Looiersgracht**, there is a congenial and well-organized little flea market at No. 38 (closed on Friday), and some attractive modern canalside architecture opposite.

57

ELANDSSTR.
PRINSENGRACHT
ELANDSGR.
OUDE LOOIERSSTR.
PRINSENGRACHT
BERENSTRAAT
WOLVENSTRAAT
KEIZERSGRACHT
RUNSTRAAT
HUIDENSTRAAT
PRINSENGRACHT
KEIZERSGRACHT
LEIDSEGRACHT

Grachtengordel/Wolvenstraat

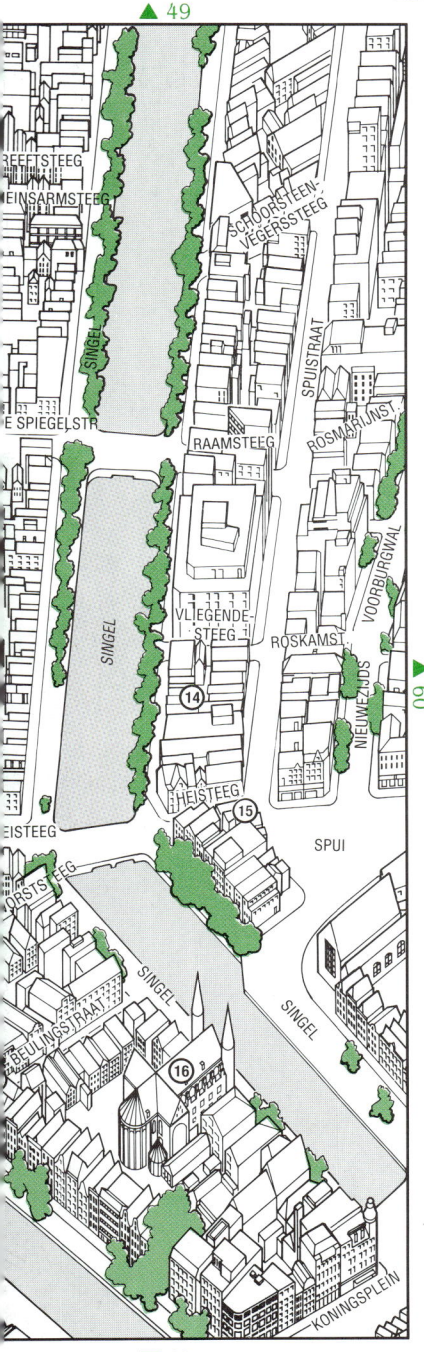

A part of the Grachtengordel (Canal Ring) which encapsulates the delights of Amsterdam, with beautiful surroundings, diverse shops and a sophisticated yet carefree atmosphere. In ① **Wolvenstraat**, notice **No. 5**, a shop front dating from 1780. At **De Knopenwinkel**, you will be tempted to buy buttons you never knew you wanted, while **Kerkhof** specializes in braid and trimmings. ② In **Runstraat** another typically individual shop is **De Witte Tanden Winkel**, entirely devoted to teeth. Indonesian restaurant **Cilubang** is always popular for its inexpensive *rijsttafel* (**f**) and **Tout Court** is one of the best French restaurants in the city (**fff**). **No. 27** is a kitsch toy shop held upright by timber posts - one of the city's many collapsing houses. ③ **Van Puffelen**: an updated brown café with, delicious food at reasonable prices and an interesting mix of faces (**ff**). In summer you can eat and drink on the barge opposite. Further along the easygoing **Prinsengracht**, look for ④ **No. 491**, a warehouse still in its original state, and ⑤ the hotel, **Wiechmann** (**ff**), which has a pretty interior and keen prices. The **Keizersgracht** here is richly ornamented. Most prominent is ⑥ the shabby **Shaffy Theater**, which began life in 1788 as the Felix Meritis (`deservedly happy') building, founded as a cultural society. Today it is once again known as the Felix Meritis Foundation, and it functions as a 'European centre for arts and sciences.' Almost opposite is ⑦ **No. 319**, classical pilasters topped by an elegant neck gable (1639). ⑧ **No. 446** is a baroque confection dating from 1725. ⑨ A splash of colour from hammock shop **Hangmatten**. ⑩ **De Admiraal**, an unusually intimate, comfortable *proeflokaal* (tasting house). ⑪ The **Ambassade**, sought-after small hotel (**ff**). ⑫ A wonderful stretch of canal houses begins with **Nos 364-370**, built in sandstone by Vingboons in 1662 and housing the **Bijbels** (Bible) **Museum**. Then comes A. Salm's overwrought copy of a New York style mansion (1890) at **Nos 380-382**. The "twins" at **Nos 390-392** depict a man and wife tied by a cord. When the marriage at No. 392 collapsed, the cord was hacked away. ⑬ The pairs of twin houses on opposite sides of the canal at **Nos 396-398** and **409-411** are known as the `brothers and sisters'. ⑭ Family-run hotel **Estheréa** (**f**). ⑮ **Hoppe**: famous brown café attracting an animated crowd which spills on to its pavement on warm evenings. ⑯ The very tall neo-Gothic church, **De Krijtberg**.

▲ 50

▲ 59

WIJDESTEEG
GAPERSTEEG
SPUISTRAAT
NIEUWEZIJDS VOORBURGWAL
ST. LUCIENSTEEG
DUIFJESSTEEG
WIJDE KAPELSTEEG
ROKIN
LOMB
CE
BROERS
KALFSV
ENGE KAPELSTEEG
KALVERSTRAAT
GEDEMPTE BEGIJNENSLOOT
ROS-MARIJNST.
BEGIJNENSTEEG
WATERSTEEG
ROSKAMST.
BEGIJNHOF
TAKSTEEG
GRIMB
SPUI
ROKIN
OUD
OLIESLAGERSST
VOETBOOGSTRAAT
HANDBOOGSTRAAT
SINGEL
SINGEL
HEILIGEWEG
KALVERSTRAAT
KLOOSTER
MU
1
2
4
5
6
7
11
12
13
14
15
17

▼70

Spui/Rokin

① You can sample almost any cuisine in **Spuistraat**: intimate **Haesje Claes** (No. 275) serves excellent Dutch food (**f**); **d'Vijff Vlieghen** (Five Flies, Nos 294-302), an antique-filled 17thC inn with a Dutch/French menu (**fff**); **Kantjil en de Tijger**, a bustling Indonesian, where the *rijsttafel* is piquant and satisfying (**f**); **Luden**, cool and modern, with brasserie food and its own café (**ff**). ② Elegant shops line **Rokin**: a huge collection of diamonds at **Amsterdam Diamond Centre** (No. 1); **Puck en Hans** (No. 66) for chic fashion; tobacconist **Hajenius** (Nos 94-6). ③ New luxury hotel, **Hotel The Grand**, in a grand 1920s town hall (**fff**). ④ In a 17thC orphanage, **Amsterdams Historisch Museum**: well-presented collection of artefacts, documents and paintings, charting the city from the 13thC: a useful place from which to start your visit to the city. The **Schuttersgalerij**, a covered passage, where the doughty faces of city burghers stare out from 17thC group portraits of the Civic Guard, is a highlight. ⑤ A refuge away from the bustle, the **Begijnhof** was founded in the 14thC to house a Catholic order of women. The simple houses enclosing the courtyard have 17thC and 18thC façades, apart from **No. 34**, the original timber house of 1460 and oldest in the city. ⑥ A clandestine **Catholic Church**, built in 1665 after Protestants requisitioned ⑦ the 15thC church, now the **English Reformed Church**. ⑧ **Huis op de drie Grachten** (House on the Three Canals, 1610), step-gabled on its three façades. ⑨ Second-hand bookstalls line **Oudemanhuispoort**. ⑩ **Grimburgwal**, a narrow street of silver-smiths. ⑪ **Athenaeum**, art nouveau bookshop with foreign publications. ⑫ **Spui**, pleasant square, centred on ⑬ **Het Lieverdje** (1960), Carel Kneulman's statue of an urchin. ⑭ **Esprit**, trendy clothes shop and café in a high-tech building. In ⑮ **Oude Turfmarkt**, old peat market, is ⑯ neoclassical **Allard Pierson Museum**, the University's archaeological collection. ⑰ Amsterdam's busiest shopping street, **Kalverstraat**, once elegant, now brash, with many chain stores. China shop **Focke & Meltzer** (No. 152) is housed in a Berlage Venetian building. A vestige of elegance is evident in the old-world department store, **Maison de Bonneterie** (No. 183). ⑱ Grand **Doelen Crest Hotel** (**fff**). ⑲ **Café de Jaren**, airy designer café. ⑳ Stylish 19thC five-star **Hotel de l'Europe** with the celebrated **Excelsior** restaurant (**fff**).

61

▲ 52

▲ 61

PRINSENHOFST.
BETHANIENSTRAAT
KOESTRAAT
KLOVENIERS STEEG
BETHANIEN-DWARSSTR.
BOERENSTEEG
OUDE HOOGSTRAAT
1
2
WALENPL.
OUDEZIJDS ACHTERBURGWAL
KORTE SPINHUISSTEEG
SPINHUISSTEEG
NIEUWE HOOGSTRAAT
12
ONKELBOEREN-STEEG
11
ZANDSTRAAT
4
ZUIDERKERKHOF
ZANDDWARSSTR.
MODDERMOLENSTRAAT
RUSLAND
3
SLIJKSTRAAT
RAAMGRACHT
RAAMGRACHT
KLOVENIERSBURGWAL
KLOVENIERSBURGWAL
KLOVENIERSBURGWAL
GROENBURGWAL
GROENBURGWAL
5
VERVERSSTRAAT
ZWANENBURGWAL
ZWANENBURGWAL
STAALSTRAAT
6
'S GRAVELANDSE VEER
STAALKADE
AMSTEL
AMSTEL

▼ 72

Jodenbuurt/Rembrandthuis

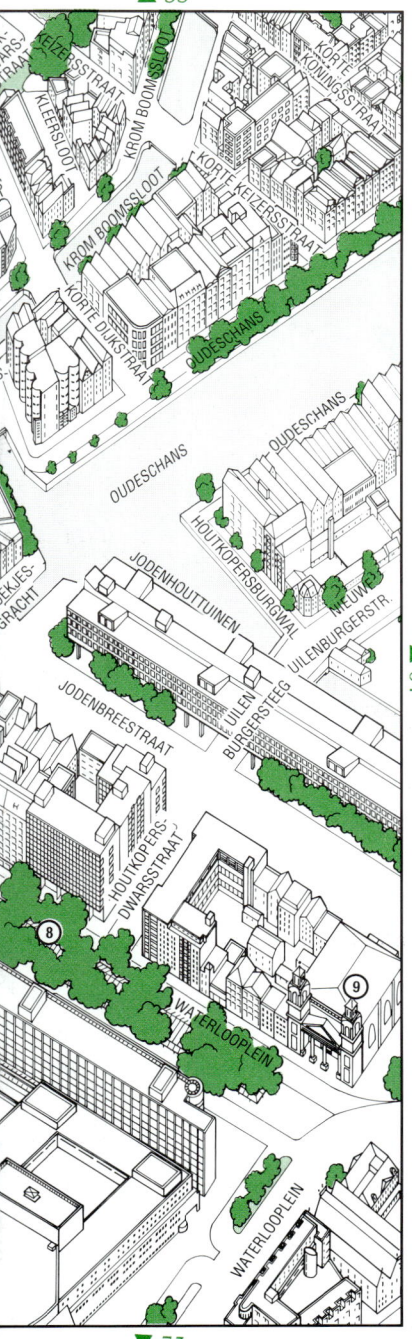

Eighty thousand Jews lived in Amsterdam before World War II, mainly in this area. By 1945, all but 5,000 were dead. Little remains of the former Jewish Quarter (Jodenbuurt) since post-war redevelopment and the building of the metro razed most of it to the ground, but there are some reminders (*see pages 55, 56 and 67*) and some signs of renewal. ① **Capsicum** sells only natural fibres - lovely silks and simple Indian cottons. Opposite is antiquarian print and bookshop, **Kok**. ② The grandiose façade of No. 29, **Trippenhuis** (1662) concealed the two separate homes of the powerful brothers Trip. They were arms dealers - hence the pair of chimneys resembling cannons. Notice, across the road, **No. 26**, a minute house said to be built with left-over stone for the Trips' coachman. ③ **SAS Royal Hotel** - modern efficiency behind two pretty 18thC doorways (**fff**). ④ With a bookish atmos-phere and regular readings, **De Engelbewaarder** has always been known as Amsterdam's literary café. Live jazz on Sundays. ⑤ No. 95, **Poppenhuis**, built by Philips Vingboons in 1642. ⑥ Tucked away, placid and pretty **Groenburgwal** is crossed with a white draw-bridge by **Staalstraat**. ⑦ The **Muziektheater** or **Stopera** building (1987), so called because it combines the Dutch *opera* and ballet companies' headquarters with the town hall (*stadhuis*), is "controversial" if you want to be polite, "hideous" if you do not. In the passage between the two buildings is the **N.A.P. Exhibition**, describing Amsterdam's extraordinary defiance of the sea, the level of which is higher than much of the city. ⑧ Waterloo-plein's long-established **flea-market** (Mon-Sat). ⑨ **Mozes en Aäronkerk** is named for the two eponymous statues on the rear wall. Now used as a space for exhibitions, concerts and meetings. ⑩ **Rembrandt-huis**, the artist's home (1639-58) during his days of prosperity, is filled with many of his magical etchings, and includes a display on the technique and its applic-ation. Opposite is the picturesque **St Antoniessluis** with its lock-keeper's cottage. Close by is **Tisfris**, a popular café at 142 St Antoniesbreestraat.No. 69, the impressive **Pintohuis**, was built in 1671. ⑪ An attractive housing complex now surrounds the **Zuiderkerk** (H.de Keyser, 1603),approached via the churchyard ⑫ In an area peppered with interesting shops, Nieuwe Hoogstraat is good for clothes and has **'t Klompenhuisje** for traditional clogs.

64

Jodenbuurt/Mr Visserplein

This lacklustre, largely unimproved area formed the poorest part of the old Jewish Quarter (Jodenbuurt, *see page 63*), a maze of tiny alleys and inferior buildings which sprang up from the beginning of the 17thC. One of the major sources of wealth and employment for the immigrant Jewish population was diamonds. They excelled at the cutting and polishing of stones (the world's largest diamond was cut here in 1912), and the city is still known as the diamond centre of the world. ① The massive Boas factory was built in 1879, contained over 350 polishing machines and employed hundreds of local workers. Now it is owned by **Gassan Diamonds** and guided tours are given. Dominating messy Mr Visserplein (named after an official who helped the Jewish people during the Occupation) is ② the bulky red-brick **Portuguese Synagogue**, built in 1675 and still the core of the small Portuguese (Sephardic) Jewish community. Across the square is the complex of Ashkenazi synagogues which now house the Joods Historisch Museum (*see page 75*). If you are walking along the Nieuwe Herengracht, look out for ③ the fine mid-18thC house at **No. 103** with its ornate entrance.

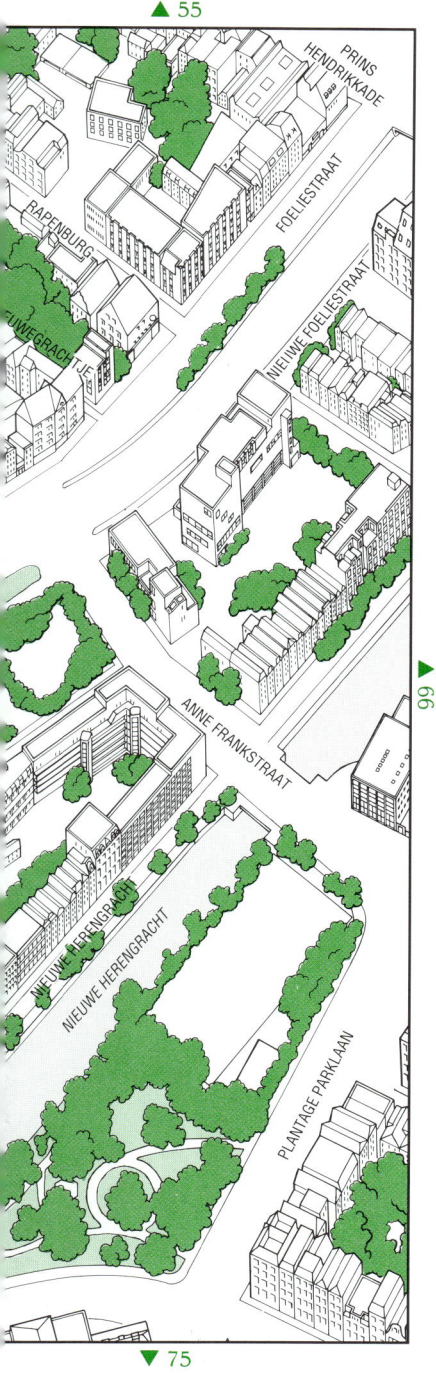

▲ 65

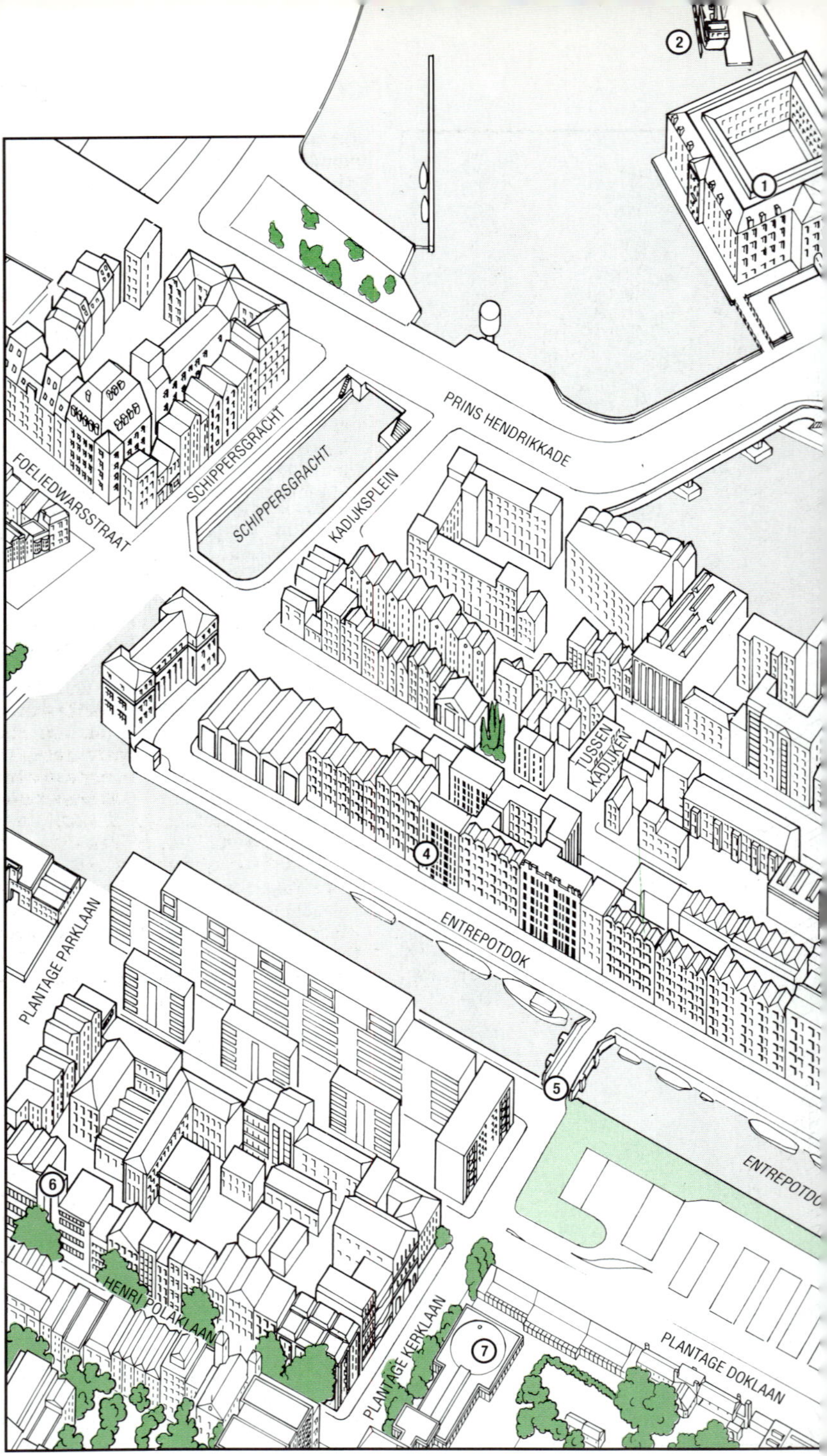
1
2
PRINS HENDRIKKADE
SCHIPPERSGRACHT
SCHIPPERSGRACHT
KADIJKSPLEIN
FOELIEDWARSSTRAAT
TUSSEN KADIJKEN
4
ENTREPOTDOK
5
ENTREPOTDOK
PLANTAGE PARKLAAN
6
HENRI POLAKLAAN
PLANTAGE KERKLAAN
7
PLANTAGE DOKLAAN

▼ 76

Entrepôtdok

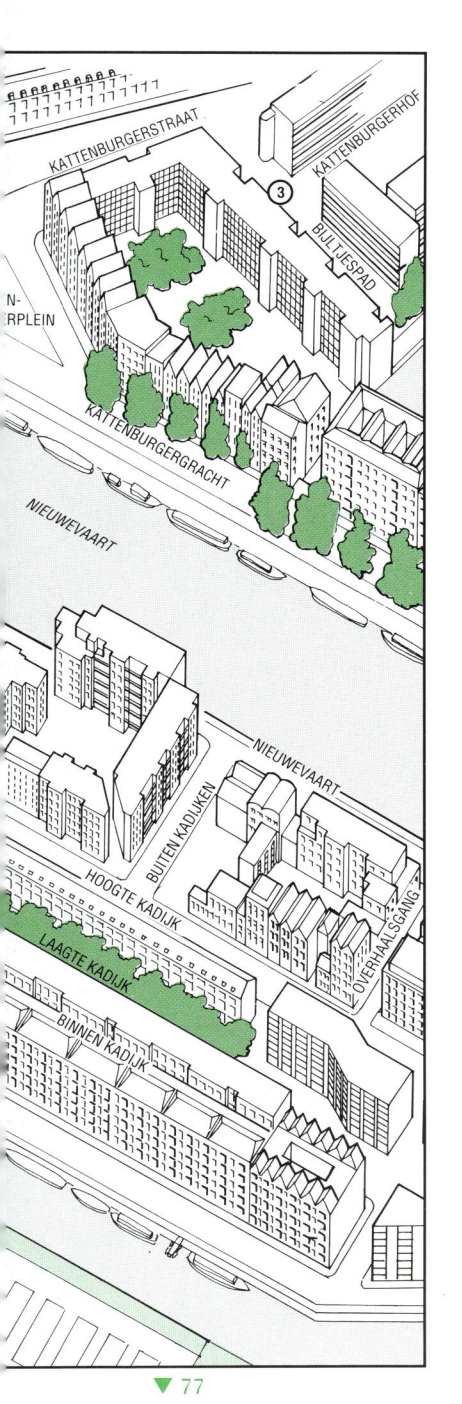

The nearby Oosterdok lends a seafaring mood to this northern section of the Plantage (see page 77). ① **Nederlands Scheepvaart Museum**. Solid and four-square, Daniel Stalpaert's imposing classical-style arsenal was built for the Admiralty in 1656, during the golden age of Dutch maritime history. Vacated by the Dutch Navy in 1971, it was converted into a museum, crammed with fascinating objects: cannons and cutlasses, instruments and maps, figureheads and anchors, paintings and meticulously accurate models, such as the three-masted, square-rigged *Drommedaris*. Don't miss the fabulous **Royal Barge** near the entrance. Labels are all in Dutch, but an English booklet is available. ② A stunning life-size replica of the 18thC East Indiaman **De Amsterdam**. With the influx of Jewish refugees from the end of the 16thC into the old docklands, the area now known as Jodenbuurt, the shipbuilding industry gradually shifted to the three Oostelijke Eilanden, which were reclaimed from marshland in 1658 by the East India Company: ③ **Kattenburg**, **Wittenburg** (off map) and **Oostenburg** (off map). Be sure to visit Stalpaert's **Oosterkerk** (25 Wittenburgergracht), now an airy and interesting exhibition centre. ④ **Entrepôtdok**, a vast development of typical 19thC warehouses, converted into offices and apartments, and incorporating several pleasant cafés and restaurants. The flat brick façades, punctuated by shuttered, arched windows, seem to stretch endlessly along the dockside; an impressive sight when viewed from ⑤ **Nijlpaardenbrug**, a toytown drawbridge, painted in primary colours. In one of the few remaining working shipyards, **Werf 't Kromhout Museum** (147 Hoogte Kadijk, off map) includes tools, machinery, steam engines, photographs of ships being built and repaired, and a slide show explaining the history of the area. ⑥ Evidence of the area's Jewish past, Berlage's **Headquarters of the Diamond Cutters' Union**, was built in 1899 in the style of an Italian *palazzo*, complete with roof-top castellat-ions and a showy entrance topped by a tower. ⑦ Inside Artis Zoo (see page 77) and covered by the same entrance ticket, the **Planetarium** takes you on a dramatic inter-galactic journey. The commentary is in Dutch, but the spectacle is worth seeing. A display in the entrance hall is concerned with meteorology, space travel and research, and the history of the planets.

▲ 58

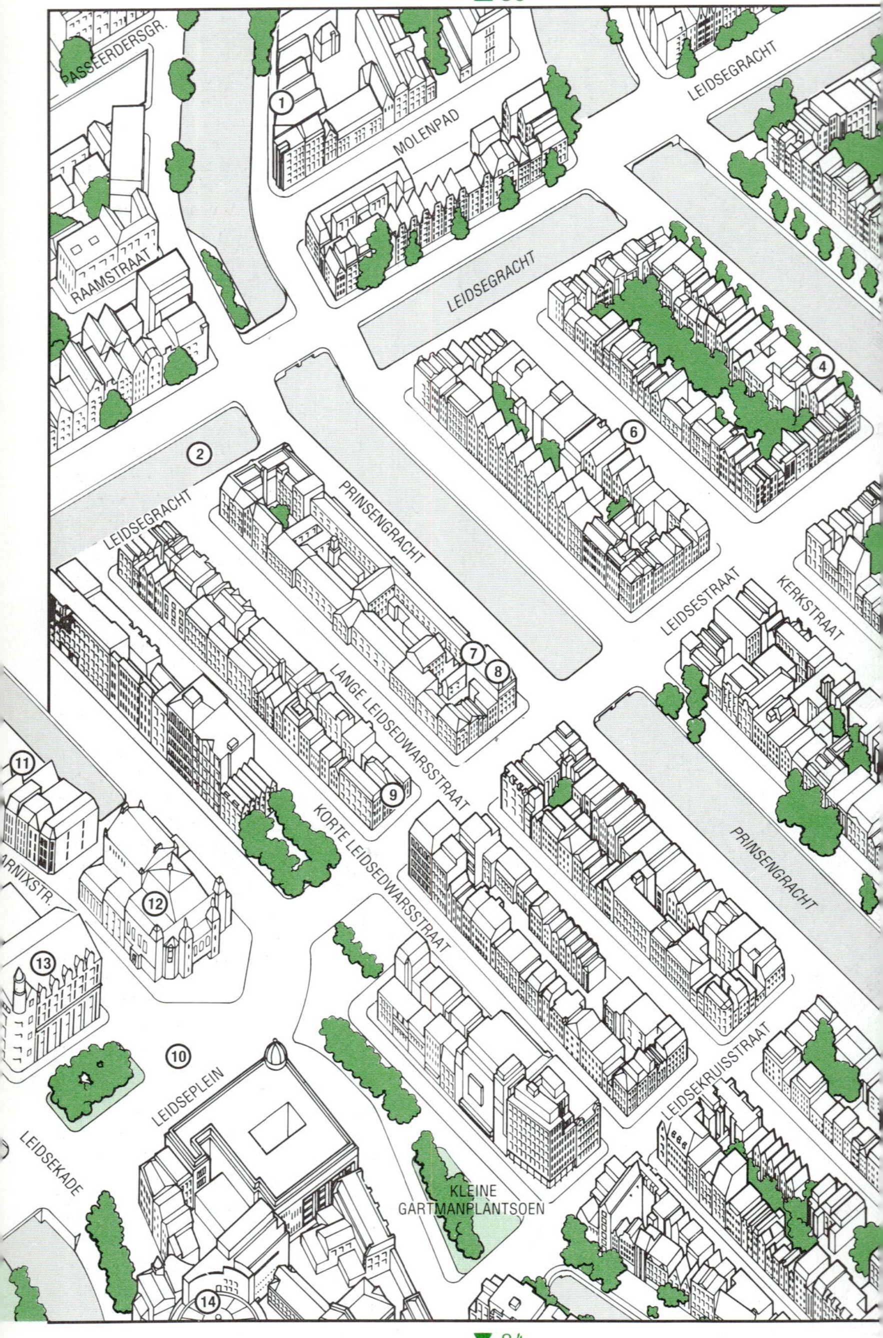
PASSEERDERSGR.
LEIDSEGRACHT
MOLENPAD
RAAMSTRAAT
LEIDSEGRACHT
LEIDSEGRACHT
PRINSENGRACHT
LEIDSESTRAAT
KERKSTRAAT
LANGE LEIDSEDWARSSTRAAT
KORTE LEIDSEDWARSSTRAAT
PRINSENGRACHT
RNIXSTR.
LEIDSEPLEIN
LEIDSEKADE
LEIDSEKRUISSTRAAT
KLEINE
GARTMANPLANTSOEN
1
2
4
6
7
8
9
10
11
12
13
14

▼ 84

Grachtengordel/Leidseplein

① **Het Molenpad**, popular brown café with a restful reading table, contemporary art on the walls, and good food (**f**). ② The lovely **Leidsegracht**, lined by canal houses in pristine condition, is Amster-dam's most prestigious address. ③ One of the first `designer' bars was **Land Van Walem**, noted for quiches and salads, and for laid-back customers (**f**). ④ **Frank Govers**, No. 500, Dutch couturier with an off-beat twist. ⑤ Founded in 1740 and now owned by Liberty of London, **Metz and Co.** sells state-of-the-art furniture. The view from the 6th floor café is over the jumble of rooftops to the Rijksmuseum, also to Westerkerk and the Jordaan. Spiral stairs lead to Gerrit Rietveld's cupola, built in 1933 and open for art exhibitions. ⑥ Amongst the many galleries in **Kerkstraat** are **Brinkman**, No. 105, current modern art, **De Witte Voet**, No. 149, current arts and crafts with an emphasis on ceramics, **Norman Automatics**, No. 153, American memorabilia that moves, **De Haas**, No. 155, art deco and nouveau and **Lambiek**, comic bookshop, No. 78. ⑦ A dedicated father and son diligently hand-paint their Delft-style pots, vases and plates in the window of their showroom, **Prinsengallerij**. ⑧ Long-established **Dikker en Thijs** now comprises two restaurants (**fff**), a brasserie (**ff**), a hotel and an excellent delicatessen. ⑨ **VVV** tourist office. ⑩ Rambling, dog-leg shaped **Leidseplein**, with a skating rink in winter (hire skates from Hoopman Bodega at No. 4), is the city's natural gathering place. Street performers, from family pop groups to lone fire-eaters keep the milling throngs amused. Fast food stalls, notably that peculiar Dutch favourite, chips with mayonnaise, proliferate. You might head for **Eijlders** (47 Korte Leidsedwarsstraat), the best café, or for the century-old **Oesterbar** (10 Leidseplein, **fff**), or **Manchurian** next door for oriental food (**ff**), or perhaps for **Bamboo Bar** (60 Lange Leidsedwarsstraat), an amiable jazz venue. ⑪ A relic of the Swinging Sixties is the multi-media **Melkweg** (Milky Way) complex, a converted dairy factory where you can watch film and music, eat, dance and buy soft drugs. ⑫ The **Stadsschouwburg** (municipal theatre) stages theatre, music and dance. ⑬ Close by is the **American Hotel** (**fff**) where, in the famous Café Américain, steep prices detract from the splendid art nouveau surroundings (W.Kromhout, 1902). ⑭ The **Lido** entertainent complex, incorporating The Casino.

▲ 60

◀ 69

12
Muntplein
KONINGSPLEIN
SINGEL
SINGEL
13
ST JORISSTRAAT
OPENHARTSTEEG
GEELVINCKSSTEEG
9
REGULIERSDWARSSTRAAT
1
HERENGRACHT
HERENGRACHT
NIEUWE SPIEGELSTRAAT
6
VIJZELSTRAAT
Museum
KEIZERSGRACHT
KEIZERSGRACHT
2
3
4
KERKSTRAAT

▼ 86

Grachtengordel/Gouden Bocht

① The much-vaunted **Gouden Bocht** (Golden Bend) of the **Grachtengordel** (Canal Ring) stretches from Leidsegracht to Vijzelstraat. But don't get too excited: here on the **Herengracht** the concentration of pompous double-width mansions built for successful bankers and merchants creates a grand but bland picture. There are eye-catchers though, particularly at **Nos 446, 475, 476, 502** (official residence of the mayor), **504-510** (wonderfully exub-erant sculpture around the neck gables), **520, 527** and **539**. ② **Nieuwe Spiegel-straat**, glowing with wealth and packed with specialist antique shops and art galleries. At **Eduard Kramer** and **M.C. Gasseling**, Nos 64 and 66, you can buy a faded antique Delft tile for as little as ten guilders or a perfect one for many hun-dreds. Next door, No. 68, **Van Os and Yu** display a wonderful collection of antique music boxes. ③ On **Keizersgracht, Nos 606-608**, looking like a pair of bewigged judges, have exceptionally tall neck gables. No. 610 lost its identical gable in 1790. ④ **Nos 672-674** were built in 1671 by Adriaen Dortsman. One is the home of the Van Loon family, and the **Van Loon Museum** (open Sun, Mon) allows a rare glimpse behind a grand façade. ⑤ The **Fodor Museum**, shows exhibitions of avant-garde, mainly Dutch, art. ⑥ Masterly, but oversized, the **A.B.N. Amro Bank**, built in 1926 by De Bazel. ⑦ **Thorbecke-plein**, a pretty square hijacked by gaudy signs and topless bars (art and craft market Sun pm). Prime Minister Thorbecke (1798-1872) turns his back, facing instead the charming **Reguliersgracht** with its seven hump-back bridges. ⑧ Delightful and excellent value, the **Seven Bridges** hotel (f). ⑨ 'Restaurant row', glitzy at night, shabby by day. There is delicious oriental food at **Dynasty** (ff), Mexican at **Rose's Cantina** (ff), dancing at the **Havana** café, gay bars at **Traffic** and **Exit**. ⑩ **Van Dobben**, for a big selection of filled rolls. ⑪ The 1921 **Tuschinski Cinema**, like a Wurlitzer just in from outer space, was the creation of its obsessive eponymous owner, who was to die at Auschwitz. The interior is a must - there are guided tours (Sun, Mon in July and Aug). Along this tacky street is a Dutch favourite, **Hema**, selling household goods and clothes at low prices. ⑫ Traffic-choked **Muntplein** is a 70-yard (65-m) wide bridge across the Singel. The **Munttoren** (Mint Tower) dates from 1619. ⑬ **Bloemenmarkt**, the beautiful floating flower market on the Singel.

▲ 62

▲ 71

AMSTEL
AMSTEL
BALK IN 'T OOGSTEEG
BAKKERSSTRAAT
ENGELSE PELGRIMSTEEG
PAARDENSTRAAT
WAGENSTRAAT
BLAUWBR
REMBRANDTSPLEIN
Rembrandtsplein
REMBRANDTSPL
AMSTELSTRAAT
1
2
3
5
9
10
HERENGRACHT
HERENGRACHT
HERENGRACHT
AMSTEL
UTRECHTSESTRAAT
REGULIERSGRACHT
KEIZERSGRACHT
KEIZERSGRACHT
KEIZERSGRACHT
KERKSTRAA

▼ 88

Grachtengordel/Amstel River

① **Rembrandtsplein** has a split personality: in the centre a tranquil garden surrounds the 19thC statue of Rembrandt, whilst around the square's sides are the trappings of a low-brow entertainment area, equal in status to the Leidseplein (*see page 68*). Cafés abound, notably **Schiller** (also a hotel, **ff**), a pre-war haunt of intellectuals. ② As the Grachtengordel (Canal Ring) makes its stately way to the Amstel, we pass **Nos 571-81 Herengracht**, four identical houses built in unison by four separate owners in 1664. The owner of No. 579 grabbed attention with a dramatic figure of archangel Michael slaying a dragon (not forgetting the elephant). ③ The **Museum Willet-Holthuysen** (No. 605) affords another chance to see inside a former canal-side residence, though it lacks the homely, lived-in feel of the Van Loon Museum (*see page 71*). A mild sense of melancholy pervades it, perhaps reflecting the lonely death of the last occupant, Louise Holthuysen, in a house overrun by cats. Her husband's collections - of ceramics, glass, silver - are on display throughout. ④ A fine, breezy stretch of the **Amstel**, which, until the construction of the Canal Ring pushed it out of focus, had been the city's *raison d'être*. ⑤ Next to **No. 216**, a splendid mansion by Adriaen Dortsman, is No. 218, the special **Six Collectie**, open only to those who have first obtained a letter of introduction from the information desk at the Rijksmuseum. It is the home of the descendants of burgomaster Jan Six, whose moving portrait by his friend Rembrandt is the family's most prized possession. Hals, Ter Borch and Saen-redam are also represented (guided tours only). ⑥ The *belle époque* opulence of the Paris-inspired **Blauwbrug** is striking, but somehow out of place. More apt is ⑦ the dainty **Magere Brug** (Skinny Bridge), the last remaining wooden drawbridge across the Amstel. ⑧ The sober **Amstelhof** was built in 1681 as an old people's home. ⑨ Bustling **Utrechtsestraat** is known for its gourmet food shops. **Sluizer** (No. 45) offers a huge choice of fish dishes in pleasantly old-fashioned surroundings (**ff**). Don't go to **Tempo Doeloe** (No. 75) unless you like it hot - if you do, *pedis* is the word to watch for on the menu (**f**). ⑩ **Kerkstraat** (*see also page 69*) was once a service street for the canal houses either side. A pleasant street to stroll in, with its long views, striking, well-restored houses, and interesting crop of galleries.

▲ 64

NIEUWE AMSTELSTRAAT

JONAS DANIEL MEIJERPLEIN

Waterlooplein

NIEUWE HERENGRACHT

DOKTER D.M. SLUYSPAD

MUIDE

NIEUWE HERENGRACHT

NIEUWE HERENGRACHT

HORTUSPLANTSOEN

▲ 73

Amstelhof

NIEUWE KEIZERSGRACHT

NIEUWE KEIZERSGRACHT

NIEUWE KEIZERSGRACHT

WEESPERSTRAAT

NIEUWE KERKSTRAAT

AMSTEL

NIEUWE PRINSENGRACHT

NIEUWE PRINSENGRACHT

AMSTEL

74

▼ 90

Weesperstraat

① Abel Cahen's prize-winning design for the **Joods Historisch Museum** (Jewish Historical Museum, 1987) perfectly marries the old - the four impressive late 17th-18thC synagogues which house it - with the new - the glass-covered street, overhead walkways and corridors that link the original buildings. The exhibition is concerned with all aspects of Judaism, and the history and culture of the Jews who settled in the Netherlands. It contains some marvellous paintings by Jewish artists, fascinating displays about the diamond industry, and brings home the true horror of the Holocaust. ② Mari Andriessen's powerful, evocative bronze statue, **De Dokwerker** (1952), a memorial to the dockers' and transport workers' strike of February 1941, which was fuelled by the deportation of over 400 Jews to death camps in retaliation for the killing of a Nazi sympathizer. Every 25 February, a ceremony is held here to commemorate the event. ③ Part of the University of Amsterdam since 1877, the **Hortus Botanicus** (Botanical Garden) dates back to 1682, when a pleasure garden, with medicinal plants and exotic species from the Dutch East Indies, was established here. Today it is a wild verdant place, dotted with ornamental lakes and tropical palmhouses, one of which contains a 400 year-old cycaspalm, the world's oldest pot plant. ④ If you are walking along **Weesperstraat** as a large boat passes up or down Nieuwe Herengracht, you will witness an amazing sight, when the entire road is raised. The quiet undeveloped banks of the Nieuwe Herengracht and Nieuwe Keizersgracht were popular sites for almshouses. Among them, ⑤ **Corvershof**, now part of Amstelhof (*see page 73*), was founded by J. Corver and S. Trip in 1723 for impoverished old couples, and is noteworthy for its arresting pediment, sculpted with allegorical figures. ⑥ **Nos 7-57 Weesperstraat**, 1960s concrete accommodation for students. ⑦ **Van Brants-Rushofje** (1732), almshouses for Lutheran women, with a handsome façade and splendid trustees' room. ⑧ **Occo's Hof** (1774), for destitute widows and spinsters, boasts another striking pediment with an eagle. ⑨ The appropriately austere, late 18thC **Luthers Verpleeghuis** (Lutheran Nursing Home). ⑩ Designed to house criminals and the destitute, **2 Roetersstraat** is now a nursing home. It has a restrained classical exterior with huge first-floor windows an airy interior.

▲ 66

▲ 75

HENRI POLAKLAAN
PLANTAGE KERKLAAN
PLANTAGE MIDDENLAAN
PLANTAGE WESTMANLAAN
PLANTAGE WESTMANLAAN
PLANTAGE MUIDERSGRACHT
PLANTAGE MUIDERGRACHT
NIEUWE PRINSENGRACHT
ROETERSSTRAAT
ACHTERGRACHT
ACHTERGR.
VALCKENIERSTRAAT
1
2
3
5

Plantage/Artis

The fourth and final extension of the crescent-shaped Grachtengordel, in 1658, took the three canals beyond the Amstel as far as the rural Plantage area. It became a popular location for old people's homes, as well as for grand second homes with expansive gardens for wealthy city dwellers. The elegant villas which characterize the area today appeared in the 19thC, many of them occupied by Jews who had prospered in the diamond industry. The horrific disappearance of the Jews from Amsterdam during the Holocaust seems all the more evil and unbelievable here in quiet, distinguished, inward-looking Plantage. ① The **Hollandse Schouwburg** (24 Plantage Middenlaan), one of several theatres in pre-war Plantage, became the main rounding-up point for Jewish families. Men, women and children were herded together here for days on end before being transported to the death camps. In the theatre's former auditorium, now a roofless cloister, a moving and little-known memorial keeps their memory alive. ② The eye-catchingly colourful **Moederhuis** (Aldo van Eyck, 1981) is a friendly environment for single mothers and their children. ③ The portal of the original 17thC almshouse has been incorporated into the beautifully rebuilt **St Jacob** old people's home. ④ **No. 6 Plantage Lepellaan** is a fine example of 19thC architecture in this area. Notice the statues which indicate a house used both in winter and summer: a man with a scythe and a woman with a cooking pot. ⑤ The **entrance** to Artis (see ⑥, this page). ⑥ If you want to give history and culture a break, while away an hour or two at Amsterdam's excellent zoo, **Artis** (full name: 'Natura Artis Magistra', meaning 'Nature, Mistress of Art'). Opened in 1838, Artis is a well-run, easy-going zoological garden where the many species of birds and animals are given plenty of space in reasonably naturalistic surroundings. Forget for a moment neck gables, the Golden Age and the Grachtengordel and watch the Japanese monkeys picking fleas off one another (and then eating them), the reptiles slithering in their steamy jungle, or the polar bears lazing with menacing unconcern. The zoo plan (in Dutch) shows places where you can shelter from the rain, one of them being the Planetarium (see page 67), another the café, and another ⑦ the **Aquarium**, a grandiose building which is home to more than 2,000 mesmerizing fish.

ENTREPOTDOK

SARPHATISTRAAT

PLANTAGE MUIDERGRACHT

MUIDERGRACHT

KAZERNESTRAAT

ALEXANDERSTRAAT

ALEXANDERPLEIN ②

ALEXANDERKADE

①

MAURITSKADE

Tropenmuseum

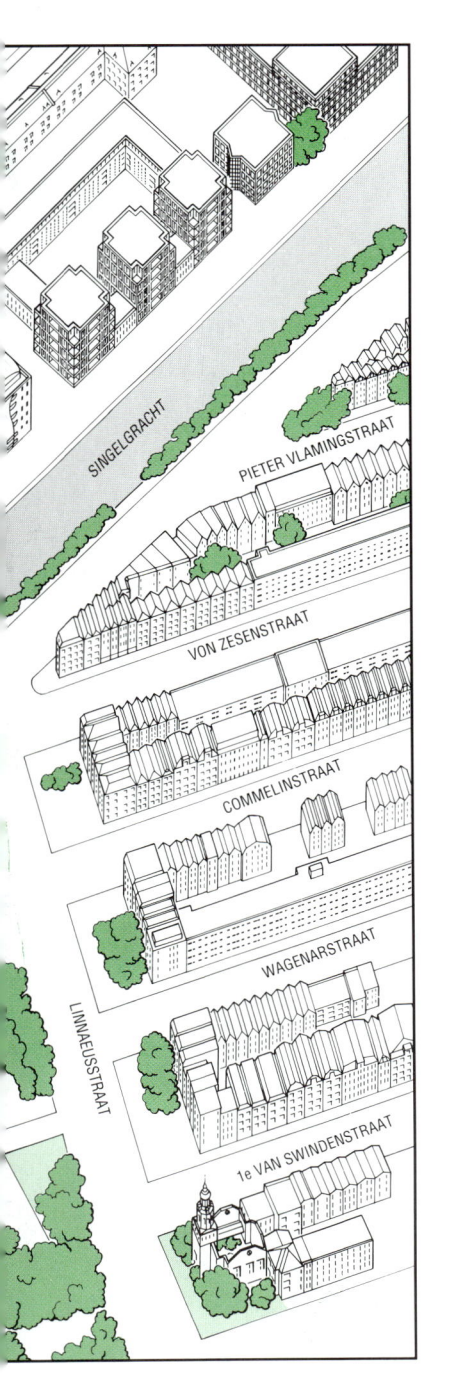

If it is still raining when you leave the zoo (*see pages 67, 77*), you can always head west along Plantage Middenlaan toward ① the **Tropenmuseum** (Tropical Museum), in an anonymous area which could be anywhere in northern Europe. However, even on a fine day it is worth a visit, and children will find plenty to amuse them. The museum is housed in the east wing of the Tropical Institute, formerly Colonial Institute, an overbearing edifice completed in 1926 when Dutch colonial interests still flourished, particularly in Indonesia. The interior is a surprise and a delight, centred on a glass-domed and galleried main hall decorated with colourful majolica. Music from the Third World is sometimes played in the hall, and temporary exhibitions are held there. The museum is organized by continent, and by themes such as music, religion and technology. The problems and pleasures of life in the developing countries are illustrated with verve by means of reconstructed streets, houses and markets, as well as superb audio-visuals and many artefacts. A separate section called T.M. Junior, is aimed at six to 12 year olds. (Closed Sat, Sun mornings). The Tropenmuseum stands opposite ② the creeper-covered former city gate, **Muiderpoort** (1770).

JELTJE DE BOSCH KEMPERPAD
ANNA SPRENGLERSTRAAT
BOEREMASTRAAT
NICOLAAS BEETSSTRAAT
BREDERODE-STRAAT
MARIUS VAN BOUWDIJK
BASTIAANSE STRAAT
1e HELMERSSTRAAT
OVERTOOM
6
ANNA VONDELSTRAAT
9
GERARD BRANDSTRAAT
VONDELST
Vondelpark
8

Vondelpark/Overtoom

① P.J.H. Cuypers' bulky brick neo-Gothic **Vondelkerk** (1872-80), dotted with turrets. Considered to be the architect's greatest achievement, it dominates the oval square he designed to accomodate it. Left empty between 1979 and 1985, it was vandalized and then, in 1986, converted into offices by A. van Stigt. Cuypers' fondness for turrets and stained glass is demonstrated by the houses at ② **No. 120** and ③ **Nos 73-75**, the back of which is covered by a glorious, rampant wistaria. ④ Cuypers lived in part (No. 77) of the double house, **Nos 77-79**, from where he could contemplate his masterpiece, the Vondelkerk. The tiled tableaux on the façade depict the architect, mason and disgruntled critic, jealous of each others' talents. ⑤ L. Royer's 1867 **statue of Joost van der Vondel**, the esteemed 17thC poet and playwright, after whom the park was named (see also page 93). ⑥ Don't miss the magnificent and totally unexpected **Hollandse Manege**. Concealed behind an unexceptional façade is a vast indoor riding school, built in 1881, with elegant plasterwork and a stunning open ironwork roof, rising high above the sand arena. If there is a lesson in progress, you can stay and watch. ⑦ Sitting happily in its verdant surroundings, looking a little like a neat beige and blue boater turned upside-down, is the round **Theehuis**, built by H.A.J. Baanders in 1936 in the New Functionalist style. Given a face-lift a few years back, it is beautifully spick and span. ⑧ An attractive if slightly derelict **bandstand**, occupying a rose-covered island in the middle of a lake. ⑨ **Hotel De Filosoof**, a small, charming, family-run hotel in a 19thC house, full of wood and stained glass, with a conservatory and pretty garden. Every room is decorated to represent a famous philosopher, from Plato to Descartes (**ff**).

VONDELSTRAAT
TESSELSCHADESTRAAT
ROEMER VISSCHERSTRAAT
1e CONSTANTIJN HUYGENSSTRAAT
VAN BAERLESTRAAT
VAN EEGHENLAAN
ALEXANDER BOERSSTRAAT
VAN EEGHENSTR
1
2
3
5
6
7
▲ 81
▼ 94

Vondelpark/P.C. Hooftstraat

Unlike the Grachtengordel (Canal Ring), this part of the city was not developed until the 19th and 20thCs, and there is a marked difference in architecture and mood.① In a glorious 19thC pavilion, **Nederlands Filmmuseum** has an exhibition devoted to the history of cinema-tography, a library of books and journals, temporary exhibitions, and film shows every evening. Within the museum, **Café Vertigo** is a trendy meeting-place with a terrace overlooking the park. ② Quiet tree-lined **Roemer Visscherstraat** has attracted a host of modest, but comfortable hotels. At No. 1, **Owl** is small and homely, with bright, attractive rooms (**f**). **Roemer Visscher** (No. 10) is larger and slightly grander, but equally friendly (**ff**). In an unusual row of houses, **Nos 20-30**, each in the architectural style of a different country and nicknamed *De Zeven Landen*, **Engeland** (No. 30A) is another charming hotel with a pretty garden (**f**). Be sure to look at **Nos 24-26**, a pink confection in the style of an Italian *palazzo*. ③ **N.J.H.C.- City Hostel Vondelpark**, youth hostel that looks more like a Swiss chalet. ④ **1- 15 Vossiusstraat**, 15 townhouses built in 1879 to resemble an 18thC palace. Cosy **Hotel Wijnnobel** occupies No. 9 (**f**). ⑤ Wander down Amsterdam's glossiest shopping street, **P.C. Hooftstraat**. There are leather goods at **Mulberry** (No. 48); china and glass at **Focke & Meltzer** (No. 67); delectable chocolates at **Drostel** (No. 92). Amongst the many fashion shops, look out for Max Mara, Gaudi (No. 116), Marc Cain (No. 84), Marina Rimaldi (No. 115), Manoukian (No. 95) and Scapa of Scotland (No. 86). Numerous cafés and restaurants make ideal lunch stops. ⑥ **Jan Luijkenstraat**, where many of the ugly 19thC buildings are now hotels. **No. 2**, built by E. Cuypers as his home, was the prototype for the Amsterdam School. ⑦ **Amsterdamse Sweelinck Conservatorium**, an imposing classical building flanked by two 17thC lions. ⑧ Even the shortest stay in this city must include a visit to the **Vincent Van Gogh Museum**, which boasts over 200 paintings and 500 drawings by this prolific artist, his letters and an exhibition of works by contemporaries. Rietveld's airy building sets off the paintings perfectly. They follow the artist's development from his murky peasant scenes, culminating in *The Potato Eaters*, to the vivid landscapes and *Vase with Sunflowers*, to the anguished last paintings, such as *Crows over the Wheatfield*.

83

▲ 68

▲ 83

KORTE LEIDSEDWARSSTRAAT
ZIESENISKADE
WETERINGSCHANS
SINGELGRACHT
STADHOUDERSKADE
VOSSIUSSTRAAT
SCHAPENBURGERPAD
PIETER CORNELIUSZ HOOFTSTRAAT
JAN LUIJKENSTRAAT
HOBBEMASTRAAT
MUSEUMSTRAAT
PAULUS POTTERSTRAAT
HONTHORSTSTRAAT
Rijksmuseum
Zuiderba
2
3
4
5
6
7

Rijksmuseum

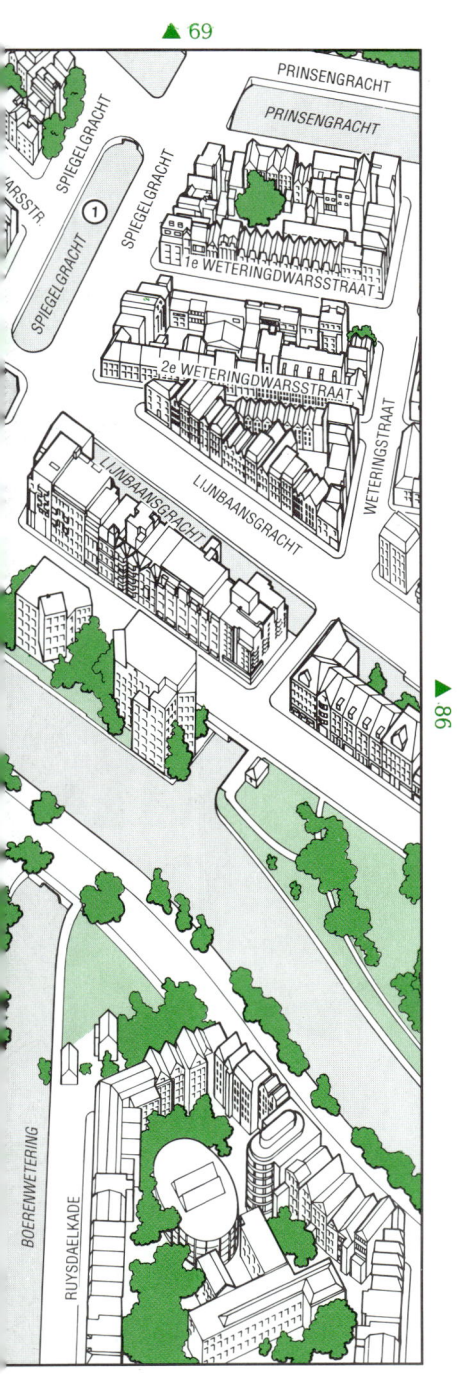

In a bold move, the Rijksmuseum was built (by P.J. Cuypers, perpetrator of the remarkably similar Centraal Station) outside the 19thC city boundaries. With an eye to the main chance, specialist antique dealers set up shop along the route to the new state museum. Nieuwe Spiegelstraat (*see pages 69, 70*) is still packed with such shops, and they spill into ① **Spiegel-gracht** (meaning mirror canal). Amongst them is bookshop **Lankamp and Brinkman** and **The Bell Tree**, stocking wooden and educational toys. ② Conn-oisseurs of rock and reggae head for **Paradiso**, a converted church, to catch interesting bands on their way to stardom. ③ It is said that the **Rijksmuseum** holds seven million treasures, yet few visitors see more than its most famous collection, the paintings of the Dutch Golden Age. All signs lead to Rembrandt's *Night Watch*, perhaps the greatest group portrait ever painted. An adjoining room is devoted to the painting, giving details in question and answer form. Leading to the *Night Watch* is the Grand Gallery, where you will pass the master's grisly *Anatomy Lesson of Dr Deyman* and his beautifully lit *Jewish Bride*. Vermeer's extraordinary handling of space, light and colour are evident in four masterpieces in Room 222, including *Young Woman Reading a Letter*, and *The Little Street*, painted from his own window. In other rooms there are a further 19 Rembrandts, unearthly church interiors by Saenredam, cattle bathed in golden light by Albert Cuyp, uproarious domestic scenes by Jan Steen, skaters by Avercamp and romantic, stormy landscapes by Ruisdael. Frans Hals, always merry, is there too, as well as tranquil Pieter de Hooch, and many other superb Dutch genre artists of the 17thC. Highlights in the rest of the museum include the 12thC *Dancing Shiva* in the Asiatic Art department, the medieval sculptures of Adriaen van Wesel (Rooms 241, 242), the furnished rooms which trace the development of Dutch interior design, and the exquisite 18thC dolls-houses (Room 162). ④ Watch a movie from the water at the atmospheric **Zuiderbad**, built in 1912. ⑤ At **Coster Diamonds** you can observe stone polish-ers at work where the Kohinoor diamond was cut for the British Crown Jewels in 1852. ⑥ **Mirafiori** has classic Italian food at surprisingly reasonable prices served in a grand pre-war setting (**ff**). ⑦ At **Sama Sebo** prices may be a little elevated, but the *rijsttafel* is unbeatable (**ff**).

▲ 70

① PRINSENGRACHT

WETERINGSTR.

1e WETERINGDWARSSTRAAT

② 2e WETERINGDWARSSTRAAT

3e WETERINGDWARSSTRAAT

NIEUWE WETERINGSTRAAT

VIJZELGRACHT

PRINSENGRACHT

③ NOORDERSTRAAT

④

VIJZELSTRAAT

▲ 85

NIEUWE VIJZELSTRAAT

WETERINGSCHANS

LIJNBAANSGRACHT

1e WETERINGPLANTSOEN

2e WETERINGPLANTSOEN

WETERINGLAAN

SINGELGRACHT

FRANS HALSSTRAAT

⑤
▼

86

Grachtengordel/Vijzelgracht

Along this stretch of the Prinsengracht, notice ① **Deutzenhofje**, Nos 855-99, elegant almshouses erected in 1695 for destitute women of the Reform church by one Agneta Deutz. One of the Prinsengracht's many art galleries, **Printshop** (No. 843), is nearby. ② The old weavers' quarter, **Weteringbuurt**, is a network of tranquil little lanes, whose names are almost as long as the streets themselves. Idiosyncratic little shops, mainly selling art and antiques, are dotted amongst the cottages. **Grill's Hofje**, with a row of nine identical bell-gables and a passage through No. 19 into the rear courtyard, is at 11-43 Eerste Weteringdwarsstraat. ③ Lunchtime at **Piet de Leeuw** finds dark-suited businessmen tucking into steak and chips in this mellow brown-walled old steakhouse (**ff**). ④ In the 1960s the old Weavers' Guild became Arthur Frommer's **Hotel Mercure**, bland but proud of its standards (**ff**). ⑤ In 1988 the Heineken brewery stopped production at this city centre plant, since it produced a mere 80,000 bottles per hour, far short of the one million bottles shot out at the company's Zoeterwoude plant. The famous tours round the white-tiled brewhouse, ending with generous helpings of free beer, ceased too, but the building, now known as the **Heineken Reception Centre**, is still open to the public. The guided tour takes about two hours, and instead of real beer production, a hi-tech audio-visual display called 'The World of Heineken' unfolds inside the five massive copper fermentation tanks. Product sampling is still part of the tour, and souvenir mugs are still presented to anyone whose birthday it is. (Mon-Fri; 18 years and over).

▲ 72

KERKSTRAAT
UTRECHTSESTRAAT
①
②
③ AMSTELVELD
PRINSENGRACHT
PRINSENGRACHT
④
REGULIERSGRACHT
⑤
⑥
UTRECHTSEDWARSSTRAAT
⑪
⑫

▲ 87
REGULIERSGRACHT

FALCKSTRAAT

HUIDEKOPERSTRAAT

⑬
⑭
FREDERI

⑯ SARPHATISTRAAT

⑮
⑰

NICOLAAS WITSENSTRAAT
PIETER PAUWSTRAAT
WESTEINDE

Grachtengordel/Frederiksplein

① Gosschalk's late 19thC Hansel and Gretel house, **Nos 57-59 Reguliersgracht**. Two houses away at **No. 63** is the English-inspired half of the pair. ② The Scandinavian Lutheran-style wooden clapboard **Amstelkerk** was built in the 17thC as a temporary Protestant church and has remained ever since. Set into the basement is the friendly modern **Café Kort**. ③ A jungle of foliage greets you on Monday mornings in **Amstelveld**, when this bland square is enlivened by a plant market. ④ A jumble of architectural styles makes this a particularly colourful stretch of the **Prinsengracht**. A smart French restaurant, **Les Quatre Canetons**, is at No. 1111 (**fff**). ⑤ Observe the pleasing lines of the 19thC neo-classical church, **De Duif**. ⑥ Gourmets and gourmands alike flock to **Utrechtsestraat** (see also pages 72, 88), a street crowded with restaurants and delis. A tempting example, **Hanssen Deli** (No. 116) is crammed with appetizing salami and a variety of teas, coffees and intriguing jars. At Nos 110-12, **A La Carte** is a shop devoted to cards, maps and travel guides. ⑦ **Amstelsluizen**, part of a network of sluice gates, closed every night so that millions of gallons of fresh water can be pumped from the IJsselmeer into the canals. ⑧ **An American Place**, steaks, burgers and other American stalwarts in a café setting (**ff**). ⑨ **Chopin**, modern piano bar with a short French menu. ⑩ **Achtergracht**, a tranquil side canal, provides a perfect mooring for houseboats. ⑪ A highly specialized gallery, **SPARTS - Art in Sports.** ⑫ **Oosterling**, authentic stone-floored café. ⑬ In this section of Reguliersgracht (see also pages 71-2, 87-8), we find **La Torre di Pisa**, redolent less of the leaning tower than of a tiny seaside restaurant, complete with fishing nets and shells (**f**). ⑭ Office workers picnic in shady **Frederiksplein**, where a fountain plays and a cylindrical ridged steel sculpture marks the 100th anniversary of Anthony Winkler Prins' encyclopedia. ⑮ Excellent *sushi* at the austerely stylish Japanese **Yoichi** (**f**). ⑯ **Sarphatistraat** takes its name from 19thC philanthropist Dr Samuel Sarphati, a key figure in the expansion of the city and building of the sensational Paleis voor Volksvlijt (Palace of National Industry), a forerunner of the Eiffel Tower, which burnt down in 1929. The site is now occupied by ⑰ the 1968 glass-clad high rise, **Nederlandse Bank**, with the nation's gold in its cellars.

▲ 74

▲ 89

LEPELSTRAAT
ONBENKENDEGRACHT
ONBENKENDEGRACHT
1
NIEUWE ACHTERGRACHT
NIEUWE ACHTERGRACHT
WEESPERSTRAAT
KORTE AMSTELSTR.
AMSTEL
AMSTEL
SARPHATISTRAAT
3
HOOLGEBRUG
PROFESSOR TULPPLEIN
HUDDESTRAAT
PROFESSOR TULPSTRAAT
4
HUDDEKADE
SINGELGRACHT
MAURITSKA
SARPHATIKADE
TORONTOBRUG
MAURITSSTRAAT
SWAMMERDAMSTRAAT
WEESPERZIJDE
AMSTELDIJK

Amstel/Sarphatistraat

Just off the map, at Nos 107-11 Amstel, is **Hotel Mikado**. It has 26 large comfortable bedrooms, most with glorious views of the river, a snug little bar and a genial atmosphere. ① It is hard to believe that the magnificent **Carré Theatre**, with its superb position on the edge of the glittering Amstel, was built at break-neck speed in 1887 to house Oscar Carré's circus. A copy of a building in Cologne, it has a fine neo-Renaissance front elevation, some splendid ironwork, and is decorated appropriately with the heads of clowns and dancers. Today, it hosts pop concerts, dance shows and lavish musicals, as well as the occasional circus. ② A 1930s glass building, the **Joodse Invalide**, now housing the Civic Health Service; notice the plaque which tells how, on 1 March, 1943, all the inhabitants of the building, who were Jewish, were taken away by the enemy. The canopied entrance echoes the roof of the pavilion perched on the top floor. An emergency medical service is now housed here. ③ **Hogesluis**, one of a series of exuberant 19thC bridges by W. Springer, influenced by the *belle époque* Alexander III bridge in Paris. ④ Emerging from its recent multi-million guilder facelift, gleaming and revitalized, the **Amstel Hotel** (**fff**) can be classed once again among the best hotels in Europe. Holland's first grand hotel, a vast edifice of yellow brick, it was built in the 1860s in French Empire style, and oozes opulence. Don't miss a peek inside at the spectacular entrance hall. Even before the renovations, when its charm had become distinctly faded, its loyal clientele of royals, tycoons and stars did not desert it. There is an excellent champagne brunch on Sundays in the **Spiegelzaal** (**ff**), and *haute cuisine* in the restaurant, **La Rive** (**fff**). In a late 19thC building by Van Gendt, who designed the Concertgebouw(*see page 95*), is a convivial café, **De IJsbreker** (23 Weesperzijde, off map). Once a welcome refuge for seamen, it was later favoured by artists, political activists and billiard-players. Although a few turn-of-the-century details remain, it has a predominantly modern interior. The building is also home to a centre for contemporary music, where internationally acclaimed musicians perform.

▲ 80

Vondelpark

① Landscaped on informal English lines in 1865-77 by J.D. and L.P. Zocher, with wide green vistas, a profusion of trees and lakes, a rose garden, teahouse and bandstand (*see page 81*), the **Vondelpark** became a Mecca for hippies in the late 1960s and 1970s, and is still a lively, colourful place, particularly on summer Sundays. Young people flock to hear open-air concerts, see a host of impromptu performers - buskers, clowns, jugglers, fire-eaters, knife-throwers - or rummage through the jumble on sale from stalls. South of the park, the streets are predominantly residential; the houses and apartment buildings only interrupted by small local shops and restaurants, of which there are a number in ② the comparatively busy thoroughfare, **Willemsparkweg**. Among them, ③ seductive antique shop **Jan Becker** boasts quality country furniture, attractive tapestry cushions, brass lamps and small bronze statues. ④ A **circus** joining Cornelis Schuytstraat with Willemsparkweg is lined with interesting shops, boutiques and restaurants: **Agora** (No. 9) is an Aladdin's cave of antique china and bric-à-brac; the florist next door **Mariade Haan** (No. 11) sells beautiful terracotta pots; **Sardegna** is a simple, but clean and inviting pizzeria at No. 17 (**f**); an excellent selection of embroidered cloth and natural-fibre woven fabric, bedspreads and clothes is available at **Vlerk** (No. 157); and at No. 177, there is a congenial neighbourhood French restaurant, **Champêtre** (**f**). The Amsterdam outpost of the famous London auctioneer **Christie's** is at 57 Cornelis Schuytstraat (off map).

▲ 82

▲ 93

Stedelijk Museum/Concertgebouw

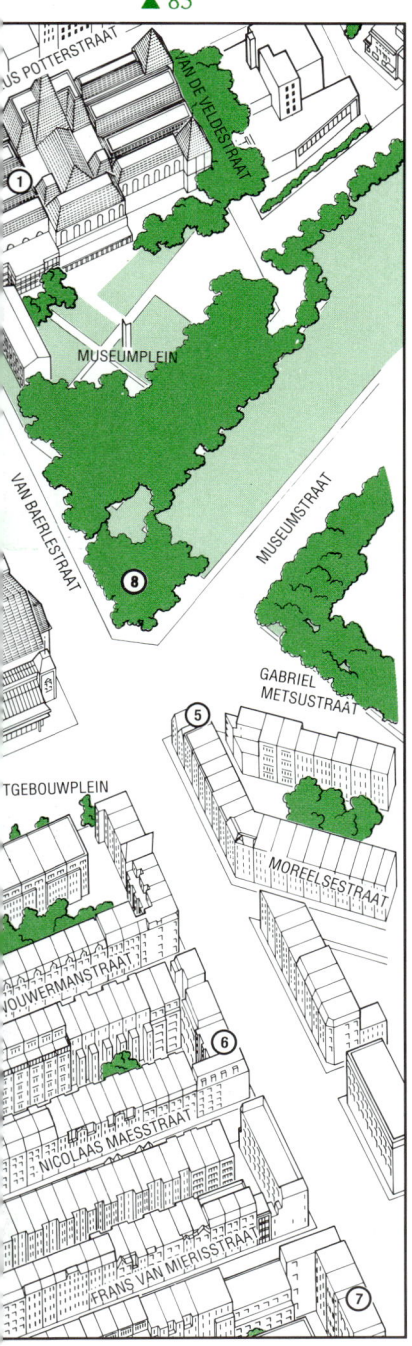

① Except in July and August, only a small part of the **Stedelijk's** collection of modern art, covering the mid-l9thC to the present day, is on view at any one time. Most of the light, white space is given over to temporary exhibitions. It is not, therefore, the place to go for an understanding of the progression of modern art, and is rather unhelpful to visitors with minimal knowledge of the subject. Instead it strives to be lively and contemporary and to show the many different faces of modern art in all its forms. It can invigorate or disappoint: collect a plan at the entrance and hope that what is on show is what you like. Some aquisitions are on almost permanent view: Matisse's *La Perruche et La Sirène;* the work of Russian artist Kasimir Malevitch which he organized especially for the museum; furniture by Gerrit Rietveld. Other artists represented by the collection include Chagall, Newman, Picasso, Beckmann, Mondriaan, and de Kooning. The museum has a popular café which overlooks the sculpture garden. ② A decade ago, the **Concertgebouw** (A.L. van Gendt, 1888) was discovered to be in danger of collapse. In time for the centenary of both concert hall and its world-famous orchestra, new foundations were laid and the building was restored and enlarged. Miraculously, all this took place without the Concertgebouw having to close. With a new conductor, Riccardo Chailly (who has had only four predeces-sors since 1888), and perfect acoustics, it remains one of the world's great concert halls. ③ **Van Baerlestraat**, stretching on past the Concertgebouw toward the Vondelpark *(pages 81, 83),* is noted for its classy stores, such as **Society, Pauw, Hobbit** (for fashions), **Van Gelder** (for crystal and porcelain), **Pisa** (for shoes), **Dik** (for jewellery), and **Palais des Parfums**. Restaurants in Van Baerlestraat include ④ **Keijzer Bodega**, where the food may not be the best, but the steady flow of musicians and media people have always given it a cachet (**fff**); ⑤ bustling French **Bartholdy** (**fff**); ⑥ longstanding **De Knijp**, comforting and unadventurous (**ff**); and ⑦ **Brasserie Van Baerle**, where you head if you wear designer clothes, paint your fingernails everyday and wear chunky gold jewellery (**fff**). ⑧ Amongst the sculpture here is the harrowing portrayal of a gypsy family, **Hel van Vuur** *(Hell of Fire,* 1978) by Heleen Levano, a memorial to all gypsies persecuted by the Nazis.

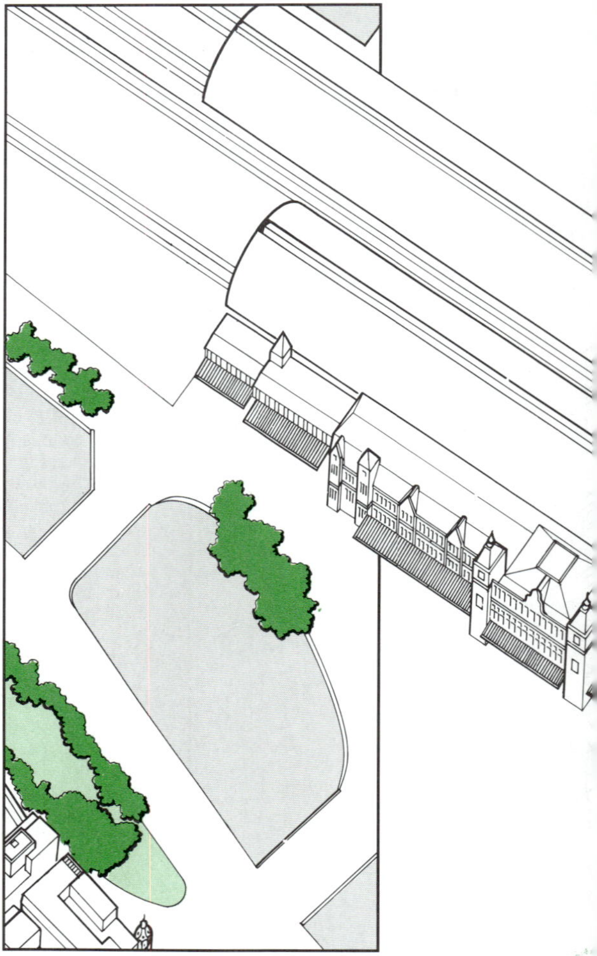

THE INDEXES

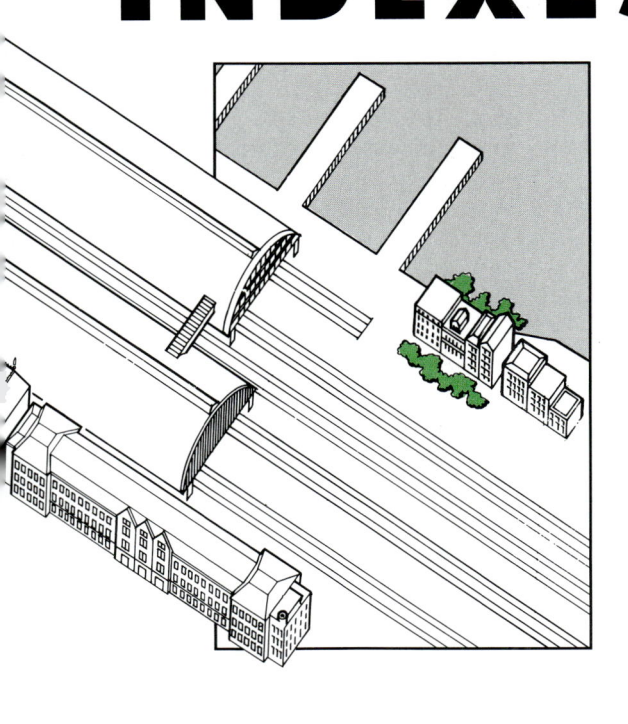

INDEX OF GENERAL POINTS OF INTEREST

A
Academy of Fine Arts 41
almshouses *see* hofjes
Alteration of 1578 53
Amstel 43, 73, 77
Amstelsluizen 89
Amsterdam, De 67
Amsterdam North 45
Amsterdam School of architecture 37, 55, 83
Anne Frank Foundation 49
Aquarium 77
art *see works of art*
Artis Zoo 67, 77

B
bandstand 81

BANKS
A.B.N. Amro Bank 71
Nederlandse Bank 89

BARS
Beiaard, De 43
Chopin 89
Exit 71
Traffic 71

INDEX OF GENERAL POINTS OF INTEREST

Beurs 51
Beurs van Berlage *see under* BUILDINGS
Bickerseiland 37
Blauwbrug 73
Botanical Garden *see* PARKS AND
   GARDENS

BROWN CAFÉS
   Bulldog 53
   Café 't Smalle 41
   Engelbewaarder, De 63
   Eijlders 69
   Hegeraad, J.A. 41
   Hoppe 59
   Molenpad, Het 69
   Nieuwe Lelie, De 47
   Papeneiland 41
   't Smackzeyl 41
   Twee Zwaantjes, De 49
   Vrouwen Café Saarein 57

Brouwersgracht 39

BUILDINGS
   No. 216 Amstel 73
   Nos 87-91 Bloemgracht 47
   No. 164 Bloemstraat 47
   No. 184 Bloemstraat 47
   No. 1 's Gravenhekje 55
   Nos 79-87 Herengracht 43
   Nos 364-370 Herengracht 59
   Nos 380-382 Herengracht 59
   No. 446 Herengracht 71
   No. 475 Herengracht 71
   No. 476 Herengracht 71
   No. 502 Herengracht 71
   Nos 504-510 Herengracht 71
   No. 520 Herengracht 71

INDEX OF GENERAL POINTS OF INTEREST

No. 527 Herengracht 71
No. 539 Herengracht 71
Nos 571-581 Herengracht 73
No. 579 Herengracht 73
No. 2 Jan Luijkenstraat 83
No. 263 Keizersgracht 49
No. 319 Keizersgracht 59
No. 446 Keizersgracht 59
Nos 606-608 Keizersgracht 71
No. 610 Keizersgracht 71
Nos 672-674 Keizersgracht 71
No. 25 Leliegracht 49
No. 103 Nieuwe Herengracht 65
No. 14 Oude Zijds Voorburgwal 53
No. 22 Oude Zijds Voorburgwal 53
No. 57 Oude Zijds Voorburgwal 53
No. 6 Plantage Lepellaan 77
No. 151 Prinsengracht 41
No. 491 Prinsengracht 59
No. 131 Prins Hendrikkade 55
Nos 57-59 Reguliersgracht 89
No. 63 Reguliersgracht 89
Nos 24-26 Roemer Visscherstraat 83
No. 7 Singel 43
No. 120 Vondelstraat 81
Nos 73-75 Vondelstraat 81
Nos 77-79 Vondelstraat 81
Nos 1-15 Vossiusstraat 83
Nos 7-57 Weesperstraat 75
No. 5 Wolvenstraat 59
Nos 2-7 Zandhoek 37
Nos 8-15 Zandhoek 37
No. 1 Zeedijk 53
A.B.N. Bank 71
Abraham and Isaac, sculptures 53
Amsterdamse Sweelinck Conservatorium 83

INDEX OF GENERAL POINTS OF INTEREST

d'Arcke Noach 43
Bartolotti House 49
Begijnhof 61
Beurs van Berlage 51
Boas factory 65
brothers and sisters 59
Concertgebouw 95
Diamond Cutters' Union,
    Headquarters of 67
Felix Meritis Foundation 59
Fortuyn, De 43
Gebouw Batavia 45
House on the Three Canals *see
    Huis op de drie Grachten,
    under* BUILDINGS
House with the Heads *see Huis
    met de Hoofden, under*
    BUILDINGS
housing block (Hembrugstraat) 37
Huis met de Hoofden 41
Huis op de drie Grachten 61
Huiszitten-Weduwenhof 41
husband and wife 59
Joodse Invalide 91
Koninklijk Paleis 51
Munttoren 71
Nederlandse Bank 89
Pintohuis 63
Politiebureau Raampoort 47
Poppenhuis 63
Post Office (Nieuwezijds
    Voorburgwal) 51
Roetersstraat nursing home 75
St Antoniessluis 63
Scheepvaarthuis 55
Spaanse Huis 43
Theehuis 81
Trippenhuis 63

INDEX OF GENERAL POINTS OF INTEREST

Westindisch Huis 43
Zeven Landen, De 83

bureau de change 45

C

CAFÉS
Artis café 77
Café Américain 69
Café de Jaren 61
Café Kort 89
Café du Lac 43
Café Vertigo 83
Esprit, L' 61
Havana 71
IJsbreker, De 91
Juriaans 41
Land Van Walem 69
Metz and Co. 69
Noord-Zuid Hollandsch Koffiehuis 45
Oosterling 89
Rooie Nelis 57
Schiller 73
Stedelijk Museum café 95
Tisfris 63
see also BROWN CAFÉS, DESIGNER CAFÉS

Canal Ring *see Grachtengordel*
car park 57
Casino, The *see Lido*
Cat Boat, The 43
children's farm 37
Chinatown 53

CHURCHES AND OTHER PLACES OF WORSHIP
Amstelkerk 89

INDEX OF GENERAL POINTS OF INTEREST

Amstelkring *see under* MUSEUMS
Catholic Church 61
Duif, De 89
English Reformed Church 61
Krijtberg, De 59
Mozes en Aäronkerk 63
Nieuwe Kerk 51
Noorderkerk 41
Oosterkerk (exhibition centre) 67
Oude Kerk 53
Portugese Synagogue 65
Ronde Lutherse Kerk 43
St Nicolaaskerk 45
Vondelkerk 81
Westerkerk 49, 69
Zuiderkerk 63

CINEMAS
Tuschinsky Cinema 71
Colonial Institute *see Tropical Institute*

CONCERT HALLS
Concertgebouw 95
Muziektheater *see Stopera*

Conservatory of Music 41

D Damrak 45

DESIGNER CAFÉS
Café de Jaren 61
IJsbreker, De 91
Land Van Walem 69

Drommedaris 67

INDEX OF GENERAL POINTS OF INTEREST

Dutch East Indies 75
Dutch West India Company 55

E Eastern Docks *see Oosterdok*
Eastern Islands *see Oostelijke Eilanden*
East India Company 67
Eigen Haard (housing project) 37
Emperors' Canal *see Keizersgracht*
Entrepôtdok 67

F ferry 45

G **GALLERIES (ART DEALERS')**
Brinkman 69
Fons Welters 47
Haas, De 69
Norman Automatics 69
Printshop 87
SPARTS - Art in Sports 89
Steendruckkerij Amsterdam 57
Witte Voet, De 69

gardens *see* PARKS AND GARDENS

GAY AMSTERDAM
Exit 71

INDEX OF GENERAL POINTS OF INTEREST

Havana (gay/straight) 71
Hotel New York 43
nightclubs 53
Traffic 71

Gentlemen's Canal *see Herengracht*
Golden Bend *see Gouden Bocht*
Gouden Bocht 71
Grachtengordel 39, 41, 43, 59, 71, 73, 77, 83

H

Haarlemmerpoort 39
hash cafés *see* Bulldog, *under BROWN CAFÉS*
Heineken Reception Centre 87
Herengracht 43

HOFJES
Amstelhof 73, 75
Anslo's Hofje 41
Bosschehofje 39
Claes Claesz Hofje 41
Corvershof 75
Deutzenhofje 87
Grill's Hofje 87
Hofje de Star 41
Huiszitten-Weduwenhof 41
Occo's Hof 75
Rapenhofje 39
St Andrieshofje 47
St Jacob 77
Suyckerhofje 41
Van Brants-Rushofje 75

INDEX OF GENERAL POINTS OF INTEREST

Zon's Hofje 41

Hogesluis 91
Hollandse Manege 81

HOLOCAUST 75, 77
    Anne Frank Huis 49
    Auschwitz 71
    dockers' and transport workers' strike 75
    effect on Jewish population 63
    gypsies, persecution and monument 95
    Hollandse Schouwburg memorial 77
    Joodse Invalide 91
    retaliatory deportation 75
    Tuschinsky 71
    see also JEWS

HOTELS
    Ambassade 59
    American 69
    Amstel 91
    Dikker en Thijs 69
    Doelen Crest 61
    Eben Haezer (youth hostel) 47
    Engeland 83
    Estheréa 59
    Europe, de l' 61
    Filosoof, De 81
    Grand Hotel Krasnapolsky 51
    Harmonie, De 89
    Holiday Inn Crowne Plaza 43
    Hotel the Grand 61
    Kabul 53
    Mercure 87
    Mikado 91

INDEX OF GENERAL POINTS OF INTEREST

New York 43
N.J.H.C.-City Hostel Vondelpark (youth hostel) 83
Owl 83
Prinsenhof 89
Pulitzer 49
Roemer Visscher 83
SAS Royal 63
Schiller 73
Seven Bridges 71
Shelter, The (youth hostel) 53
Singel 43
Sonesta 43
Wiechmann 59
Wijnnobel 83

I

IJsselmeer 89

J

JEWS, HISTORY OF IN AMSTERDAM
    arrival in Amsterdam 67
    diamond industry 65, 67, 75, 77
    Frank, Anne 49
    Jewish Historical Museum *see Joods Historisch Museum, under* MUSEUMS
    Jewish Quarter *see Jodenbuurt, under* JEWS
    Jodenbuurt 55, 63, 65, 67
    Joods Historisch Museum *see under* MUSEUMS

INDEX OF GENERAL POINTS OF INTEREST

Joodse Invalide 91
Pintohuis 63
Plantage, growth of 77
population 63
Portugese Synagogue 65
Sarphati, Dr Samuel 89
Sephardic community 65
Visser, Mr 65
see also HOLOCAUST

Jordaan 39, 41, 69

K Keizersgracht 43
Kattenburg 67

L left luggage facilities 45
Lido entertainment complex 69
Louise-Bewaarschool (No. 151 Prinsengracht) *see under* BUILDINGS
Lutheran Nursing Home *see Luthers Verpleeghuis*
Lutheran Orphanage 43
Luthers Verpleeghuis 75

INDEX OF GENERAL POINTS OF INTEREST

M

Magere Brug 73

MARKETS
    Amstelveld plant market 89
    Antiekmarkt De Looier 57
    art and craft market 71
    bird market 41
    Bloemenmarkt 71
    Boerenmarkt 41
    flea markets 57, 63
    Nieuwmarkt 53
    Noordermarkt 41
    Westerstraat 41

Melkweg 69
Milky Way complex *see Melkweg*
Mint Tower *see Munttoren, under*
    BUILDINGS
Moederhuis 77
Montelbaanstoren 55
Muiderpoort 79
Municipal Transport Authority 55

MUSEUMS (INCLUDING PUBLIC ART GALLERIES)
    Allard Pierson Museum 61
    Amsterdams Historisch Museum 61
    Anne Frank Huis 49
    Bible Museum *see Bijbels Museum, under MUSEUMS*
    Bijbels Museum 59
    Fodor Museum 71
    Joods Historisch Museum 65, 75
    Madame Tussaud Scenerama 51
    Museum Amstelkring 45, 53
    Museum Willet-Holthuysen 73
    N.A.P. Exhibition 63

INDEX OF GENERAL POINTS OF INTEREST

Nederlands Filmmuseum 83
Nederlands Scheepvaart Museum 67
Nederlands Theater Museum 49
Rembrandthuis 63
Rijksmuseum 45, 69, 85
Schuttersgalerij 61
Six Collectie 73
Stedelijk Museum 95
T.M. Junior *see Tropenmuseum*
Tropenmuseum 79
Tropical Museum *see Tropenmuseum, under* MUSEUMS
Van Loon Museum 71, 73
Vincent Van Gogh Museum 83
Werf 't Kromhout Museum 67

MUSIC VENUES
Bamboo Bar 69
Joseph Lam Jazzclub 37
Melkweg 69
Paradiso 85

N New York (USA) 43
Nijlpaardenbrug 67

INDEX OF GENERAL POINTS OF INTEREST

O
Oostelijke Eilanden 67
Oostenburg 67
Oosterdok 45, 67
Oosterkerk (exhibition centre) 67

P
Paleis voor Volksvlijt 89

PARKS AND GARDENS
Hortus Botanicus 75
Vondelpark 81, 83, 93

Planetarium 67, 77
Plantage 67, 77
Poezenboot, De 43
police station 57

POST OFFICES
Postkantoor (Zaanstraat) 37
Stationspostgebouw 55

Prinseneiland 37
Prinsengracht 39

PROEFLOKALEN
Admiraal, De 59
Café t'Smalle (café) 41
Drie Fleschjes, De 51

public transport information 45

INDEX OF GENERAL POINTS OF INTEREST

R

Realeneiland 37

RESTAURANTS
American Place, An 89
Bartholdy 95
Bols Taveerne 47
Bordewijk 41
Brasserie Van Baerle 95
Centra 53
Champêtre 93
Chopin 89
Christophe' 49
Cilubang 59
Dikker en Thijs 69
Dikker en Thijs (brasserie) 69
Dynasty 71
Excelsior 61
Gouden Reael, De 37
Grand Café Ie Klas 45
Groene Lantaarn, De 47
Haesje Claes 61
Kantjil en de Tijger 61
Keijzer Bodega 95
Kikker, De 41
Knijp, De 95
Luden 61
Manchurian 69
Mirafiori 85
Noord-Zuid Hollandsch Koffiehuis 45
Oesterbar 69
Piet de Leeuw 87
Port van Cleve, Die 51
Quatre Canetons, Les 89
Rive, La 91
Rose's Cantina 71
Rum Runners 49
Sama Sebo 85

INDEX OF GENERAL POINTS OF INTEREST

    Sardegna 93
    Sea Palace Restaurant 55
    Seven Seas, The 43
    Silveren Spiegel, De 43
    Sluizer 73
    Sonesta Hotel 43
    Speciaal 47
    Spiegelzaal 91
    Stuivertje, Het 57
    Tempo Doeloe 73
    Torre di Pisa, La 89
    Tout Court 59
    Treasure 51
    Van Harte 49
    Van Puffelen 59
    Vijff Vlieghen, d' 61
    Yoichi 89

River IJ 45
rijsttafel 47, 59, 61, 85
Roetersstraat nursing home *see under*
    BUILDINGS

Royal Barge 67

S Schipperskinderenschool 43
    Schreierstoren 45
    sculptures *see* STATUES AND SCULPTURES

    SHOPS AND STORES
      Agora 93
      A La Carte 89
      Allert de Lange 51
      Amsterdam Diamond Centre 61
      Ariège, Jacques d' 83

INDEX OF GENERAL POINTS OF INTEREST

Athenaeum 61
Baobab 57
Becker, Jan 93
Bell Tree, The 85
Bijenkorf, De 51
Bonebakker 61
Bop Street 47
Cain, Marc 83
Capsicum 63
cheese shop (Prinsengracht) 39
Christie's 93
Condomerie Het Gulden Vlies 53
Coster Diamonds 85
Dikker en Thijs 69
Drostel 83
Electric Lady 47
English Bookshop, The 57
Esprit 61
Focke & Meltzer 61, 83
Gassan Diamonds 65
Gasseling, M.C. 71
Gaudi 83
Govers, Frank 69
Haan, Mariade 83
Haasje, 't 57
Hajenius 61
Hangmatten 59
Hanssen Deli 89
Hema 71
Hobbit 95
Kef, Robert & Abraham 57
Kerkhof 59
Klompenhuisje, 't 63
Knopenwinkel, De 59
Kok 63
Kramer, Eduard 71
Lambiek 69
Lankamp and Brinkman 85

INDEX OF GENERAL POINTS OF INTEREST

Liberty 69
Maghreb, Al 47
Maison de Bonneterie 61
Manoukian 83
Mara, Max 83
Metz and Co. 69
Mulberry 83
Palais des Parfums 95
Pauw 95
Peek and Cloppenburg 51
Pisa 95
Prinsengallerij 69
Puck en Hans 61
Rimaldi, Marina 83
Rinascimento 49
Scapa of Scotland 83
second-hand bookstalls 61
silversmiths 61
Sisters 57
Society 95
Spitsbergen 39
Terra 49
toy shop (Runstraat) 59
Van Dobben 71
Van Gelder 95
Van Os and Yu 71
Varenkamp 49
Vlerk 93
Vliegende Kikker, Die 47
Vos, Edgar 83
Wijs & Zonen 53
Witte Tanden Winkel, De 59

Singel 43
skating rink 69
Stadhuis (town hall) *see Stopera*

INDEX OF GENERAL POINTS OF INTEREST

STATIONS
Centraal Station 37, 45, 85

Stationsplein 45

STATUES AND SCULPTURES
Dokwerker, De (Andriessen) 75
Frank, Anne 49
Hel van Vuur (Levano) 95
Lieverdje, Het (Kneulman) 61
Nationaal Monument 51
Rembrandt 73
steel cylinder (Prins' monument) 89
Thorbecke, Prime Minister 71
Vondel, Joost van der (Royer) 81
Stock Exchange (1903) *see Beurs van Berlage, under* BUILDINGS

Stock Exchange *see Beurs*
Stopera 63
tasting houses *see* proeflokalen

T

THEATRES
Carré Theatre 91
Hollandse Schouwburg 77
Municipal Theatre *see Stadsschouwburg, under* THEATRES
Muziektheater *see Stopera*
Shaffy Theater 59
Stadsschouwburg 69

town hall *see Stopera*
tourist information 45, 69
Tropical Institute 79

U University of Amsterdam 75

W Waag 53
Walletjes, De 53
Westelijke Eilanden 37
Westerkanaal 37
Westerdok 37
Western Dock *see Westerdok*
Western Islands *see Westelijke Eilanden*
Weteringbuurt 87
white cafés *see designer cafés*
Wittenburg 67

Z Zoutkeetsgracht 37
Zuiderbad 85

INDEX OF NAMES OF PEOPLE

A
Alexander III
    bridge (Paris) 91
Andriessen, Marie 75
Arkel, van 49

B
Baanders, H.A.J. 81
Beatrix, Queen 51
Berlage, H.P. 51, 61
Bonaparte, Louis 51
Bonaparte, Napoleon 51
Brecht 51
Brod 51

C
Cahen, Abel 75
Campen, Jacob van 51
Carré, Oscar 91
Chailly, Riccardo 95
Corver, J. 75
Cuyp, Albert 85
Cuypers, E. 83
Cuypers, P.J.H. 45, 81, 85

INDEX OF NAMES OF PEOPLE

D
De Bazel 71
Deutz, Agneta 87
Dortsman, Adriaen 43, 71, 73
Dussel, Mr 63

E
Eyck, Aldo van 77

F
Frank, Anne 49, 63
    statue 49
Frommer, Arthur 87

G
Gerritszoon, Ivo 47
Gosschalk 89
Greef, B. de 47

H
Hals, Frans 73, 85
Hartman, Jan 53
Holthuysen, Louise 73
Hooch, Pieter de 85
Hoppe, Pieter 41
Hudson, Henry 45
Keyser, Hendrick de 41, 49, 55, 63, 71

INDEX OF NAMES OF PEOPLE

K Keyser, Pieter de 41, ?49
Klerk, Michel de 37, 55
Kneulman, Carel 61
Kramer, P.L. 55
Krasnapolsky 51
Kromhout, Willem 69

L Levano, Heleen 95

M Malevitch, Kasimir 95
Matisse, Henri 95
Mey, Johan van der 55

P Pinto 63
Prins, Anthony Winkler 89

Q Quellinus, Artus, the Elder 51

R Raep, Pieter Adriaensz 39
Rietveld, Gerrit 69, 83, 95
Rembrandt van Rijn 47, 53, 63, 73, 85
   statue 73

INDEX OF NAMES OF PEOPLE

Royer, L. 81
Ruisdael 85
Ruyter, Admiral de 55

S Saenredam 73, 85
Salm, A. 57
Sarphati, Dr Samuel 89
Six, Jan 73
Springer, W. 91
Staal, J.F. 91
Staets, Hendrick 43
Stalpaert, Daniel 41, 67
Steen, Jan 85
Stigt, A. van 81

T Ter Borch 73
Thorbecke, Prime Minister 71
    statue 71
Trip, brothers 63
Trip, S. 75
Tuschinski 71

V Van Gendt, A.L. 91, 95
Van Gogh, Vincent 55, 83
Van Loon, family 71
Vermeer 53, 85
Vingboons, Philips 49, 57, 63
Viollet-le-Duc 45
Visserplein, Mr 65

INDEX OF NAMES OF PEOPLE

Vondel, Joost van der 81
  statue 81

W   Wesel, Adriaen van 85

Z   Zocher, J.D. 93
Zocher, L.P. 93

INDEX OF STREET NAMES

A
Achtergracht 76
Achter Oosteinde 89
Akoleienstraat 46
Alexander Boersstraat 82, 94
Alexanderkade 78
Alexanderplein 78
Alexanderstraat 78
Amstel 62, 71, 72, 73, 74, 89, 90
Amsteldijk 90
Amstelstraat 72
Amstelveld 88
Anjeliersdwarsstraat, 1e 40
Anjeliersdwarsstraat, 2e 40
Anjeliersstraat 40
Anna Sprenglerstraat 80
Anne Frankstraat 65
Anna Vondelstraat 80

B
Baanbrugsteeg 38
Bakkersstraat 72
Balk in 't Oogsteeg 72
Banstraat 93, 94

INDEX OF STREET NAMES

Barentszplein 37
Barentszstraat 36
Barndesteeg 52
Begijnensteeg 60
Begijnhof 60
Berenstraat 58
Bergstraat 49, 50
Bethaniendwarsstraat 62
Bethanienstraat 52, 62
Beulingstraat 59
Beursplein 51
Beursstraat 51, 52
Bickersgracht 37, 39
Bijltjespad 67
Binnen Bantammerstraat 53
Binnen Brouwersstraat 42
Binnen Dommersstraat 38
Binnengasthuisstraat 61
Binnen Kadijk 67
Binnenkant 53, 54
Binnen Oranjestraat 39
Binnen Visserstraat 42
Binnen Wieringerstraat 42
Blauwbrug 72
BlauwburgWal 42, 50
Blindenmansteeg 71
Bloedstraat 52
Bloemdwarsstraat, 1e 47
Bloemdwarsstraat, 2e 46
Bloemgracht 46, 48
Bloemstraat 47, 48
Blokmakerstraat 39
Boeremastraat 80
Boerensteeg 62
Boerhaavestraat, 1e 91
Boerhaavestraat, 2e 91
Bokkinghangen 37
Boomdwarsstraat, 1e 40

INDEX OF STREET NAMES

Boomdwarsstraat, 2e 40
Boomsteeg 52
Boomstraat 40
Brandewijnsteeg 53
Brederodestraat 80
Breeuwersstraat, 1e 36
Breeuwersstraat, 2e 36
Brouwersgracht 38, 39, 41, 42
Buiten Bantammerstraat 54
Buiten Brouwersstraat 42
Buiten Dommersstraat 38
Buiten Kadijken 67
Buiten Oranjestraat 39
Buiten Visserstraat 43
Buiten Wieringerstraat 42

C

Cellebroerssteeg 60
Commelinstraat 79
Concertgebouwplein 95
Constantijn Huygensstraat, 1e 82
Constantijn Huygensstraat, 2e 81
Cornelis Schuytstraat 92

D

Da Costastraat 56
Dam 50
Damrak 44, 51, 52
Damraksteeg 50

INDEX OF STREET NAMES

Damstraat 51
De Lairessestraat 93, 94
Den Texstraat 87
De Ruijterkade 44
Dijkdwarsstraat 63
Dijkstraat 52, 63
Dirk Hartoghstraat 36
Dirk van Hasseltssteeg 50
Dokter D.M. Sluyspad 74
Driehoekstraat 38
Driekoningenstraat 49
Droogbak 43
Dubbeleworststeeg 59
Duifjessteeg 60

E
Egelantiersdwarsstraat, 1e 40
Egelantiersdwarsstraat, 2e 40
Egelantiersgracht 40, 46, 47, 48
Egelantiersstraat 40, 46
Eggerstraat 50
Elandsgracht 57, 58
Elandsstraat 56, 58
Elleboogsteeg 52
Emmastraat 92
Enge Kapelsteeg 60
Enge Kerksteeg 52
Enge Lombardsteeg 61
Engelse Pelgrimsteeg 72
Entrepôtdok 66

INDEX OF STREET NAMES

F
Falckstraat 88
Focke Simonszstraat 87
Foeliedwarsstraat 66
Foeliestraat 65
Frans Halsstraat 86
Frans van Mierisstraat 95
Frederiksplein 88

G
Gabriel Metsustraat 95
Galgenstraat 36
Gapersteeg 60
Gasthuismolensteeg 49
Gebed Zonder End 60
Gedempte Begijnensloot 60
Geelvinckssteeg 70
Geldersekade 52, 53
Gerard Brandstraat 80
Goudsbloemdwarsstraat, 1e 38, 40
Goudsbloemdwarsstraat, 2e 38, 40
Goudsbloemdwarsstraat, 3e 40
Goudsbloemstraat 38, 40
Gouwenaarssteeg 43
's Gravelandse Veer 62
's Gravenhekje 54
Gravenstraat 50
Grimburgwal 60
Groenburgwal 62
Groenmarktkade 56
Grote Bickersstraat 37

INDEX OF STREET NAMES

H   Haarlemmerdijk 39
Haarlemmer Houttuinen 38, 42
Haarlemmerplein 38
Haarlemmerstraat 42
Halvemaansteeg 71
Handboogstraat 60
Haringpakkerssteeg 44
Hartenstraat 48
Hasselaerssteeg 44
Hazenstraat 57
Heiligeweg 60
Hekelveld 43
Heintje Hoeksteeg 52
Heisteeg 59
Helmersstraat, 1e 80
Hendrik Jonkerplein 39
Henri Polaklaan 66, 76
Herengracht 42, 49, 58, 59, 69, 70, 72
Herenmarkt 42
Herenstraat 41, 42
Hermietenstraat 50
Hobbemakade 85
Hobbemastraat 84
Hondecoeterstraat 94
Honthorststraat 83, 84
Hoogte Kadijk 67
Hoolgebrug 90
Hortusplantsoen 74
Houtkopersburgwal 63
Houtkopersdwarsstraat 63
Houtmandwarsstraat 36
Houtmankade 36
Houtmanstraat 36
Huddekade 90
Huddestraat 90
Hugo de Grootstraat, 1e 46
Huidekoperstraat 88

INDEX OF STREET NAMES

Huidenstraat 58

J Jacob Obrechtstraat 94
Jac. Oliepad 39
Jan Luijkenstraat 83, 84
Jan Willem Brouwersstraat 94
J.B. Siebbeleshof 63
Jeltje de Bosch Kemperpad 80
Jeroenensteeg 43
Jodenbreestraat 63, 64
Jodenhouttuinen 63, 64
Johannes Verhulststraat 93, 94
Jonas Daniel Meijerplein 64, 74
Jonge Roelensteeg 50

K Kadijksplein 66
Kalfsvelsteeg 60
Kalkmarkt 54
Kalverstraat 50, 60
Karnemelksteeg 44
Karthuizersdwarsstraat 40
Karthuizersplantsoen 40
Karthuizersstraat 40
Kattenburgergracht 67
Kattenburgerhof 67
Kattenburgerplein 67
Kattenburgerstraat 67
Kattengat 43

INDEX OF STREET NAMES

Kazernestraat 78
Keizerrijk 50
Keizersgracht 41, 42, 48, 58, 69, 70, 72
Keizersstraat 53, 63
Kerkstraat 68, 70, 72, 87, 88
Kinkerstraat 56
Kleersloot 63
Kleine Bickersstraat 37
Kleine Gartmanplantsoen 68
Klimopweg 43
Klooster 60
Kloveniersburgwal 52, 61, 62
Kloveniersteeg 62
Koestraat 52, 62
Koggestraat 43
Kolksteeg 51
Konijnenstraat 57
Koninginneweg 92
Koningslaan 92
Koningsplein 59, 69, 70
Koningsstraat 53
Korsjespoortsteeg 42
Korte Amstelstraat 90
Korte Dijkstraat 63
Korte Keizersstraat 63
Korte Kolksteeg 43
Korte Koningsstraat 53, 63, 64
Korte Korsjespoortsteeg 42
Korte Leidsedwarsstraat 68, 84
Korte Lepelstraat 75
Korte Lijnbaanssteeg 50
Korte Marnixkade 38
Korte Marnixstraat 38
Korte Niezel 52
Korte Prinsengracht 39, 42
Korte Reguliersdwarsstraat 71
Korte Spinhuissteeg 62

INDEX OF STREET NAMES

Korte van Eeghenstraat 94
Korte Wagenstraat 38
Kreupelsteeg 52
Krom Boomssloot 53, 63
Kromme Palmstraat 38
Kromme Waal 53

L Laagte Kadijk 67
Lange Leidsedwarsstraat 68, 85
Lange Niezel 52
Langestraat 42
Lastageweg 53
Laurierdwarsstraat, 1e 46, 57
Laurierdwarsstraat, 2e 47
Laurierdwarsstraat, 3e 56
Lauriergracht 47, 48, 56, 57
Laurierhof 47
Laurierstraat 47, 48, 56
Leidekkerssteeg 51
Leidsegracht 58, 68
Leidsekade 68
Leidsekruisstraat 68
Leidseplein 68
Leidsestraat 68, 69
Leliedwarsstraat, 1e 48
Leliedwarsstraat, 2e 47
Leliedwarsstraat, 3e 46
Leliegracht 48
Lepelkruisstraat 75
Lepelstraat 90
Lijnbaansgracht 38, 46, 56, 85, 87
Lijnbaanssteeg 50
Lijnbaansstraat 56

INDEX OF STREET NAMES

Lindendwarsstraat, 1e 40
Lindendwarsstraat, 2e 40
Lindengracht 39, 40
Lindenstraat 40
Linnaeusstraat 79
Looiersdwarsstraat, 1e 57
Looiersdwarsstraat, 2e 57
Looiersdwarsstraat, 3e 56
Looiersgracht 57

M Maarten Janszen Kosterstraat 89
Magere Brug 73
Mandenmakerssteeg 51
Manegestraat 74
Marius van Bouwdijk Bastiaanse
　Straat 80
Marnixkade 46
Marnixplantsoen, 2e 46
Marnixstraat 38, 46, 56, 68
Martelaarsgracht 44
Matrozenhof 66
Mauritskade 78, 90
Mauritsstraat 90
Meester Visserplein 64
Minnemoersstraat 39
Moddermolenstraat 62
Molenpad 68
Molensteeg 52
Molsteeg 50
Monnikenstraat 52
Montelbaanstraat 53, 54
Moreelsestraat 95
Mosterdpotsteeg 50

INDEX OF STREET NAMES

Mouthaansteeg 38
Mozes en Aaronstraat 50
Muiderstraat 64, 74
Muntplein 60
Museumplein 83, 95
Museumstraat 84, 95

N Nadorststeeg 50
Nassaukade 46, 56
Nes 50, 60
Nicolaas Beetsstraat 80
Nicolaas Maesstraat 95
Nicolaas Witsenkade 87
Nicolaas Witsenstraat 87, 88
Nieuwe Achtergracht 75, 90, 91
Nieuwe Amstelstraat 64, 73, 74
Nieuwe Batavierstraat 64
Nieuwebrugsteeg 44, 52
Nieuwe Doelenstraat 61
Nieuwe Egelantiersstraat 46
Nieuwe Foeliestraat 65
Nieuwegrachtje 65
Nieuwe Herengracht 65, 73, 74
Nieuwe Hoogstraat 62
Nieuwe Houttuinen 38, 39
Nieuwe Jonkerstraat 53, 54
Nieuwe Keizersgracht 73, 74
Nieuwe Kerkstraat 73, 74, 75
Nieuwe Leliestraat 47, 48
Nieuwe Looiersdwarsstraat 86
Nieuwe Looiersstraat 87
Nieuwendijk 43, 44, 50
Nieuwe Nieuwstraat 50

INDEX OF STREET NAMES

Nieuwe Prinsengracht 74, 75, 76
Nieuwe Ridderstraat 53, 54
Nieuwe Spaarpotsteeg 50
Nieuwe Spiegelstraat 69, 70
Nieuwe Teertuinen 36
Nieuwe Uilenburgerstraat 63, 64
Nieuwevaart 67
Nieuwe Vijzelstraat 86
Nieuwe Wagenstraat 38
Nieuwe Weteringstraat 86
Nieuwezijds Armsteeg 43
Nieuwezijds Kolk 43, 50
Nieuwezijds Voorburgwal 43, 50, 59, 60
Nieuwmarkt 52
Noorderdwarsgracht 86
Noordermarkt 41
Noorderstraat 86
Norderkerkstraat 40

O Olieslagerssteeg 60
Onbekendegracht 90
Onkelboerensteeg 62
Onze Lieve Vrouwesteeg 51
Oosteinde 89
Oosterdokskade 54
Oostersekade 64
Openhartsteeg 70
Oude Brugsteeg 51, 52
Oude Hoogstraat 62
Oudekennissteeg 52
Oude Kerksplein 52

INDEX OF STREET NAMES

Oude Leliestraat 49
Oude Looiersstraat 57, 58
Oudemanhuispoort 61
Oude Nieuwstraat 42
Oudeschans 54, 63, 64
Oude Spiegelstraat 59
Oude Turfmarkt 60
Oude Waal 53, 54
Oudezijds Achterburgwal 52, 61, 62
Oudezijds Armsteeg 52
Oudezijds Kolk 45, 52
Oudezijds Voorburgwal 51, 52, 61
Overhaalsgang 67
Overtoom 80

P Paardenstraat 72
Paleisstraat 49, 50
Palestrinastraat 94
Palmdwarsstraat 38
Palmgracht 38
Palmstraat 39
Panaalsteeg 43
Papenbrugsteeg 50
Passeerdersdwarsstraat, 1e 57
Passeerdersgracht 57, 68
Passeerdersstraat 57
Paternostersteeg 51
Paulus Potterstraat 83, 84, 95
Pentagon 62
Peperstraat 55, 64
Pieter Corneliusz Hooftstraat 83, 84
Pieter Jacobszdwarsstraat 51
Pieter Pauwstraat 88

INDEX OF STREET NAMES

Pieter Vlamingstraat 79
Pijlsteeg 51
Planciusstraat 36
Plantage Badlaan 77
Plantage Doklaan 66, 77
Plantage Kerklaan 66, 76
Plantage Lepellaan 76
Plantage Middenlaan 75, 76
Plantage Muidergracht 75, 76, 77, 78
Plantage Parklaan 65, 66, 75
Plantage Westmanlaan 76
Prinseneiland 36, 39
Prinsengracht 40, 41, 48, 57, 58, 68, 69, 85, 86, 87, 88
Prinsenhofsteeg 61, 62
Prinsenstraat 41
Prins Hendrikkade 43, 44, 45, 53, 54, 55, 65, 66
Professor Tulpplein 90
Professor Tulpstraat 90

R Raadhuisstraat 48, 49, 50
Raamgracht 62
Raamsteeg 59
Raamstraat 68
Ramskooi 44
Rapenburg 54, 65
Rapenburgerstraat 64
Realengracht 36
Recht Boomssloot 53, 54, 64
Reestraat 48
Reguliersbreestraat 71
Reguliersdwarsstraat 70

INDEX OF STREET NAMES

Reguliersgracht 71, 72, 87, 88
Reguliersteeg 71
Rembrandtsplein 72
Rijnspoorplein 91
Roemer Visscherstraat 82
Roetersstraat 76
Roggeveenstraat 36
Rokin 50, 60
Romeinsarmsteeg 59
Roomolenstraat 42
Roskamsteeg 59, 60
Rosmarijnsteeg 59, 60
Rozendwarsstraat, 1e 47
Rozendwarsstraat, 2e 46
Rozengracht 47, 48
Rozenstraat 47, 48, 56
Runstraat 58
Rusland 61, 62
Ruysdaelkade 85

S
Sarphatikade 89, 90
Sarphatistraat 77, 78, 88, 90, 91
Schapenburgerpad 83, 84
Schapensteeg 71
Schippersgracht 66
Schippersstraat 54
Schoorsteenvegerssteeg 59
Schoutensteeg 51
Servetsteeg 51
Singel 42, 43, 49, 50, 59, 60, 70
St Agnietenstraat 61
St Annendwarsstraat 52
St Annenstraat 51, 52

INDEX OF STREET NAMES

St Antoniesbreestraat 52, 62
St Barberenstraat 61
St Geertruidensteeg 50
St Jacobsstraat 43
St Jansstraat 51
St Jorisstraat 70
St Luciensteeg 60
St Nicolaasstraat 50
St Olofspoort 44
Slijkstraat 61, 62
Sloterdijkstraat 36
Smaksteeg 43
Smidssteegje 53
Snoekjesgracht 63
Snoekjessteeg 63
Spaarpotsteeg 50
Spiegelgracht 85
Spinhuissteeg 62
Spinozastraat 91
Spooksteeg 52
Spui 59, 60
Spuistraat 43, 49, 50, 59, 60
Staalkade 62
Staalstraat 62
Stadhouderskade 83, 84, 89
Stationsplein 44
Steenhouwerssteeg 51
Stoofsteeg 52
Stormsteeg 52
Stromarkt 43
Suikerbakkerssteeg 50
Swammerdamstraat 90

INDEX OF STREET NAMES

T
Taandwarsstraat 37
Taanstraat 37
Taksteeg 60
Teerketelsteeg 42
Tesselschadestraat 82
Thorbeckeplein 71
Tichelstraat 40
Torensteeg 49, 50
Torontobrug 90
Treeftsteeg 59
Tuindwarsstraat, 1e 40
Tuindwarsstraat, 2e 40
Tuinstraat 40
Turfdraagsterpad 61
Tussen Kadijken 66

U
Uilenburgersteeg 63
Utrechtsedwarsstraat 88
Utrechtsestraat 72, 88

V
Valckenierstraat 76, 91
Valeriusstraat 93
Valkenburgerstraat 64
Valkensteeg 50
Van Baerlestraat 82, 95
Van Breestraat 93, 94
Van der Veldestraat 82, 95
Van Eeghenlaan 82, 94
Van Eeghenstraat 82, 92, 94

INDEX OF STREET NAMES

Van Heemskerckstraat 36
Van Linschotenstraat 36
Van Neckstraat 37
Van Noordtkade 36
Van Swindenstraat, 1e 79
Vendelstraat 61
Verversstraat 62
Vierwindendwarsstraat 36
Vierwindenstraat 36
Vijzelgracht 86
Vijzelstraat 70, 86
Vinkenstraat 38
Violettenstraat 40
Vliegende Steeg 59
Voetboogstraat 60
Vondelstraat 80, 82
Von Zesenstraat 79
Vossiusstraat 83, 84
Vredenburgersteeg 52

W Waalsteeg 53
Wagenaarstraat 79
Wagenstraat 72
Walenpleintje 62
Wanningstraat 94
Warmoesstraat 44, 51, 52
Waterlooplein 63, 73
Watersteeg 60
Weesperstraat 74, 90
Weesperzijde 90
Westeinde 88
Westerkade 46
Westermarkt 48

INDEX OF STREET NAMES

Westerstraat 40
Weteringdwarsstraat, 1e 85, 86
Weteringdwarsstraat, 2e 85, 86
Weteringdwarsstraat, 3e 86
Weteringlaan 86
Weteringplantsoen, 1e 86
Weteringplantsoen, 2e 86
Weteringschans 84, 86, 87
Weteringstraat 85, 86
Wibautstraat 91
Wijde Heisteeg 59
Wijde Kapelsteeg 60
Wijde Kerksteeg 52
Wijde Lombardsteeg 60
Wijdesteeg 60
Wijngaardsstraatje 52
Willemsparkweg 93, 94
Willemsstraat 38
Wolvenstraat 58
Wouwermanstraat 95

Z
Zanddwarsstraat 62
Zandhoek 37
Zandpad 83
Zandstraat 62
Zeedijk 44, 52
Zeilmakerstraat 39
Zieseniskade 84
Zoutkeetsgracht 36
Zoutkeetsplein 36
Zoutsteeg 50
Zuiderkerkhof 62
Zwanenburgwal 62
Zwarte Handsteeg 50

AMSTERDAM PUBLIC TRANSPORT MAP

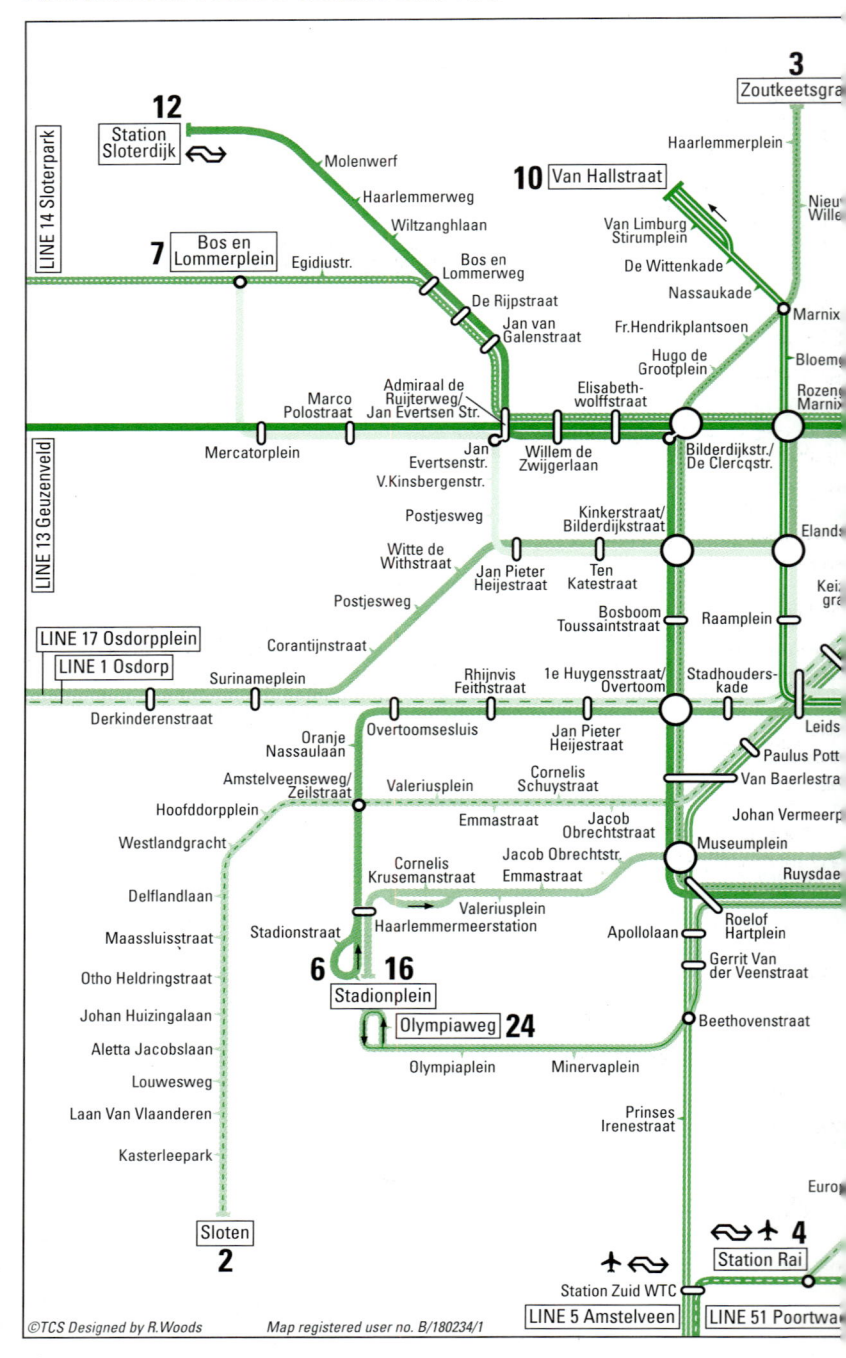

LINE 14 Sloterpark

12 Station Sloterdijk

3 Zoutkeetsgra

Molenwerf
Haarlemmerplein

Haarlemmerweg

10 Van Hallstraat

Wiltzanghlaan

Van Limburg Stirumplein

Nieu Wille

7 Bos en Lommerplein

Egidiustr.

Bos en Lommerweg

De Wittenkade

De Rijpstraat

Nassaukade

Marnix

Jan van Galenstraat

Fr. Hendrikplantsoen

Hugo de Grootplein

Bloeme

Marco Polostraat

Admiraal de Ruijterweg/ Jan Evertsen Str.

Elisabethwolffstraat

Rozeng Marnix

Mercatorplein

Jan Evertsenstr. V.Kinsbergenstr.

Willem de Zwijgerlaan

Bilderdijkstr./ De Clercqstr.

LINE 13 Geuzenveld

Postjesweg

Kinkerstraat/ Bilderdijkstraat

Elands

Witte de Withstraat

Jan Pieter Heijestraat

Ten Katestraat

Kei: gra

Postjesweg

Bosboom Toussaintstraat

Raamplein

LINE 17 Osdorpplein
LINE 1 Osdorp

Corantijnstraat

Rhijnvis Feithstraat

1e Huygensstraat/ Overtoom

Stadhouderskade

Surinameplein

Derkinderenstraat

Overtoomsesluis

Leids

Oranje Nassaulaan

Jan Pieter Heijestraat

Paulus Pott

Amstelveenseweg/ Zeilstraat

Valeriusplein

Cornelis Schuystraat

Van Baerlestra

Hoofddorpplein

Emmastraat

Jacob Obrechtstraat

Johan Vermeerp

Westlandgracht

Cornelis Krusemanstraat

Jacob Obrechtstr. Emmastraat

Museumplein

Ruysdae

Delflandlaan

Valeriusplein

Roelof Hartplein

Maassluisstraat

Stadionstraat

Haarlemmermeerstation

Apollolaan

Gerrit Van der Veenstraat

Otho Heldringstraat

6   **16**

Johan Huizingalaan

Stadionplein

Beethovenstraat

Aletta Jacobslaan

Olympiaweg **24**

Louwesweg

Olympiaplein

Minervaplein

Laan Van Vlaanderen

Prinses Irenestraat

Kasterleepark

Euro

Sloten
2

✈ ⇌   **4** Station Rai

Station Zuid WTC

LINE 5 Amstelveen   **LINE 51 Poortwa**

©TCS Designed by R.Woods   Map registered user no. B/180234/1

142

AMSTERDAM PUBLIC TRANSPORT MAP

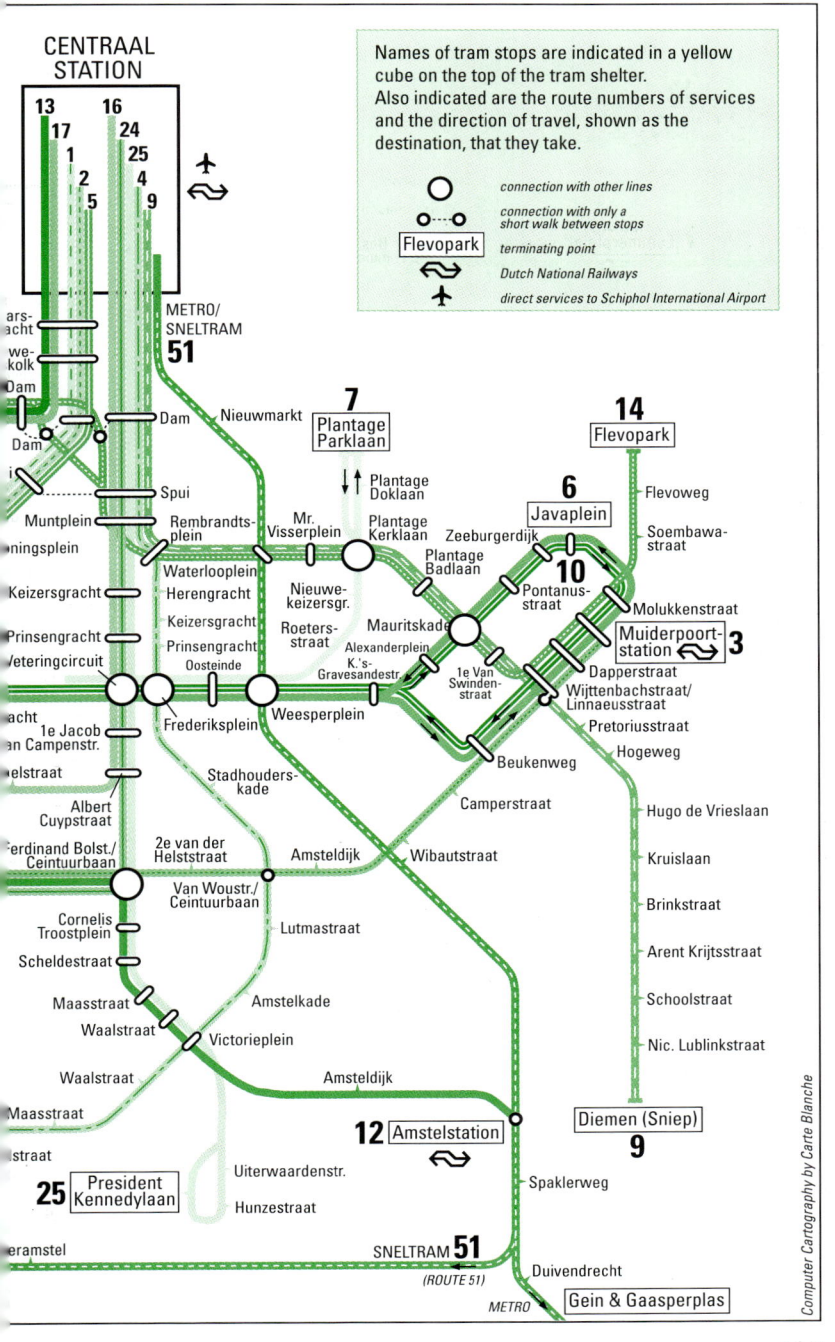